WRITING EROTIC FICTION

and getting published

Mike Bailey

TEACH YOURSELF BOOKS

Long renowned as the authoritative source for self-guided learning – with more than 30 million copies sold worldwide – the *Teach Yourself* series includes over 200 titles in the fields of languages, crafts, hobbies, sports, and other leisure activities.

A catalogue record for this title is available from The British Library

Library of Congress Catalog Card Number on file.

First published in UK 1997 by Hodder Headline Plc, 338 Euston Road, London NW1 3BH

First published in US 1998 by NTC Publishing Group
An imprint of NTC/Contemporary Publishing Company
4255 West Touhy Avenue, Lincolnwood (Chicago), Illinois 60646•1975 U.S.A.

The 'Teach Yourself' name and logo are registered trade marks of Hodder & Stoughton Ltd in the UK.

Typeset by Hart McLeod, Cambridge.
Printed in England by Cox & Wyman Limited, Reading, Berkshire.

Impression number   10 9 8 7 6 5 4 3 2 1
Year   2000 1999 1998 1997

CONTENTS

ACKNOWLEDGEMENTS

With thanks to the following writers: Bethany Amber, Rebecca Ambrose, Aaron Amory, Felice Ash, Samantha Austen, Tom Crewe, Georgina Brown, Amelia Greene, Cheryl Mildenhall, Brian Levy and Nina Sheridan.

Also to Ian Covell, Barbara Levy, Bill Massey, James Michael and Bob Tanner.

And a particular thank you to Sue Welfare and Sue Dyson for their advice.

Acknowledgement is also made to Headline Book Publishing for permission to use the statistics from the Delta erotic survey.

FOREWORD

Question: What's the difference between erotica and
          pornography?

Answer: Erotica is what turns me on, pornography is
          what turns on the dirty old man next door.

The modern erotic novel is a new kid on the block. Only in the past
two decades have booksellers felt free to offer openly for sale novels of
an explicitly sexual nature. Of course, the pornographic novel has a
long and dishonourable history and its now-legitimate offspring has a
recognised place on the shelves – in fact, novels of this kind have rows
of shelves all to themselves. They wouldn't be there if they didn't sell.

This guide is intended to help writers who would like to write one of
this new breed of pornographic novel. Many fine books of instruction
already exist to help the mainstream novelist and what they say is of
just as much relevance to the erotic writer. However, there are areas
of specific interest to the latter and I'll try to concentrate on them –
the parts that other literary guides don't reach.

My qualifications for offering advice on this subject are that I've
written a few of these contemporary erotic novels and I've published
lots, as the editor of Star Books for W.H. Allen, then Nexus for Virgin
and currently Delta and Liaison for Headline. These are not the only
kind of books that I edit but the genre has expanded so much of recent
years that I spend more and more time in the mansion of Eros.

Come inside. Leave your literary inhibitions at the door and, please,
don't forget your sense of humour – it's the most essential credential
of all.

1
THE BASICS

'Love is not the dying moan of a distant violin – it's the triumphant twang of a bedspring.'

S. J. Perelman

What is an erotic novel?

That's a tricky question. It's not *Lady Chatterley's Lover* or *Ulysses* or *Lolita* – to name three controversial works of twentieth century literature. Nor is it a novel by Harold Robbins or Jackie Collins or Jilly Cooper – or any number of contemporary commercial novelists who are perceived as 'sexy' writers. Though sexual behaviour is at the heart of these books and erotic sequences part of the reading experience, explicit sex is only one ingredient among many that makes them successful.

For the purposes of this guide, an erotic novel is one designed specifically to inspire the reader's sexual imagination. If it fails in that primary purpose, no matter how successful it may be in other areas, then it fails completely. A good erotic novel should arouse you like a lover – or at least like an efficient striptease artist. If the juice does not flow, you do not pass Go.

'I see no reason in morality (or in aesthetic theory) why literature should not have as one of its intentions the arousing of thoughts of lust. It is one of the effects, perhaps one of the functions of literature to arouse desire.'

Lionel Trilling

Novels of this nature have been written and published in English since the mid-eighteenth century. The most infamous of all, John Cleland's *Memoirs of a Woman of Pleasure* [*Fanny Hill*], appeared within a decade of Samuel Richardson's *Pamela* (1740/1) – the first recognised novel in the English literary canon. Until recently, Fanny and her sisterhood were banned. Generations of writers and publishers operated in secret, under threat of prosecution, and an entire category of fiction was dismissed as corrupting filth.

Now this underground river of erotic creativity has surfaced and flows legitimately into every bookshop in the land. As such, sexy novels published by the likes of Nexus, Delta, Black Lace, X Libris, Silver Moon, Masquerade, Liaison – the list grows long – comprise a new genre. Only in the past ten years or so have such original works found their way on to open sale. We now have a proliferation of imprints dedicated to erotic fiction and an established market in the book trade. At a conservative guess, approximately three to four hundred new novels are published every year in the UK and the USA. Even the snootiest bookshops are designating specific shelves to 'Erotica' and booksellers say that no one – man, woman or maiden aunt – is embarrassed to pick them up. The literary outcast has at last been allowed in out of the cold.

In our terms then, an erotic novel is a work of genre fiction designed to titillate the reader sexually and as legitimate a bookshop purchase as any other. And you want to write one. Read on.

Are you sitting comfortably?

'A surprising number of writers feel silly about writing sex scenes.'

Lesley Grant-Adamson
Teach Yourself Crime and Suspense Fiction (1996)

I assume that if you are serious about writing an erotic novel you are not one of these writers. I can remember a long-ago conversation with a friend when I told him I was trying to write a novel (a navel-gazing, post-adolescent-angst kind of thing). He said, 'Great, but how do you deal with *sex*?' and the way he said it, in tones of pure terror, stuck in my mind. My friend would have died rather than describe the act of making love.

There's no room for modesty here. If the notion that your readers may be physically affected by what you write embarrasses you, abandon the idea of writing erotica now. As has already been established, the purpose of these books is to turn people on. If you are successful, some readers will drag their partners into bed when they get home from work – or simply hold the book in one hand and pleasure themselves with the other. Novels of this nature are the original one-handed read and if you shrink from that then your literary ambitions should be aimed in another direction.

Conversely, you may find the idea that you can have such an effect on the lives of your readers pleasing. After all, it is a rare novel that can have a physical consequence on the person who reads it. If you make a good job of it then your book should do just that.

Erotic survey: How did you come by this book?

Female respondent: With my fingers!

The word and the flesh

'The subject of erotic literature is an area of our lives that exists within us like a separate, troubled country. Like Death, sex obsesses us all in ways we often cannot define or admit, even to ourselves... The function of erotic literature is to express the secret part of our lives which periodically rules us no less than money or death.'

Michael Perkins, *The Secret Record* (1976)

Reading fiction – any popular fiction – brings us face to face with situations that would appal and terrify us in real life. To look through the eyes of Clarice Starling into the face of Hannibal Lecter, to choose like Sophie on the platform at Auschwitz which of your children will die, to stand over a mound of frozen corpses in the Moscow winter cold with a secret policeman at your side – how many of us would actually want to experience events such as these? But in reading popular novels like Thomas Harris's *The Silence of the Lambs*, William Styron's *Sophie's Choice* and Martin Cruz Smith's *Gorky Park* we can of course participate in safety. What's more we can look our worst nightmare in the eye and see it off. In novels, we know that virtue will vanquish, truth will out and love will conquer all. A satisfying blockbuster read gives us all the reassurance of a religion that promises life after death. And, like a mother with a sick child, the novelist says to us, 'Despite the many terrible things that I've shown you in my story, everything's going to be all right.' And we believe her.

What then of erotica, this bastard offspring born out of literary wedlock, whose respectability many would still dispute? What is the erotic novelist's underlying message?

Erotica, as much if not more than any other genre, offers vicarious thrills. It gives us licence to explore a hedonistic wonderland where the usual social conventions do not apply. In these books, the fabulous flesh of fantasy men and women is displayed solely for our carnal appreciation. To borrow from Henry Miller, this is the Land of Fuck and here we can have who we want as often as we like – without even paying for dinner. What's more, we can let our libidos off the leash and go for a walk on the wild side. It is unlikely, if the opportunity arose, that many of us would stroll down the Champs Elysées in nothing but a pair of high heels or join the cast of a blue movie on a Greek island or agree to become a sex slave to an Italian diva in return for singing lessons. But these and myriad other titillating possibilities beckon from the bookshelves. And – to credit the examples I've cited – readers of Nicole D's *The Sex Diary of Nicole Dupont*, Susan Sebastian's *Island in the Sun* and Rebecca Ambrose's *Queen of the Night* have only to turn the pages to share the experience.

Like popular fiction, sexually explicit novels also offer a reassuring message, aimed at the pleasure-seeker in us all. They promise that the hedonist will outwit the killjoy, that the sublime joys of sex will be worth all sacrifices and that the realities of life – mortality, taxes, ugliness, drudgery – will pale before the momentary ecstasy of carnal delight. Except that, in these books, such delight is not momentary. In both practical and symbolic terms, the orgasm in erotica is a tidal wave, each succeeding thrill bigger and more enduring than the last.

Erotic novels seek to enlarge the elusive moments of sexual bliss that make up the generality of our sexual experience. They magnify sensual pleasure at the expense of all other emotions. Characters in erotica never say, 'Later, darling' – they cry, 'I want it now!' Significant events can take place in erotic novels – war, revolution, plague – but the most significant is always the protagonist's next fuck. This may be a daft way of looking at the world but no one ever had a reasoned argument with a man sporting an erection. And that is who you, the novelist, are addressing – a sexually aroused reader who, as such, has a different world view and priorities to one who is not. That reader is like an impatient lover. He or she has expectations and it is up to you as the author to fulfil them.

How erotica is read

Don't kid yourself that readers dwell on the scene-setting or the evocation of a sunset before the protagonists retire for the night. It used to be that people read novels looking for 'the dirty bits' and skipping pages until they got to them. That was before explicit erotica was on open sale. In erotic fiction there should be no need to skip, as the dirty bits are guaranteed to arrive before the reader has to go in search of them. Elmore Leonard was not referring to erotica when he said, 'I try to leave out the parts that people skip' – but you should be.

Are you up to it?

Having established precisely the nature of the book we are discussing and that you are comfortable with the idea of writing one – what next?

First, a word of warning. Erotic fiction requires the same degree of literacy as any other kind. The tools of your trade are those used by the recognised masters of the novel from Austen to Amis. Like all novelists, you must be able to create an imaginary world by skilful wordplay. Contrary to what many people think, to write a successful erotic novel you must be able to write.

That sounds obvious but it's worth thinking about in connection with genre erotic fiction. An erotic novel of 75,000 to 80,000 words requires more than sex. The author must invent an ambience for the reader and fill it with character, incident and atmosphere. In other words, you've got to be able to tell a tale on paper. If you cannot write a sentence that conveys the precise meaning you intend, then you are in trouble.

Just because you are writing about sex does not mean you can get away with sloppy prose, illogical plotting and schoolboy howlers. Just because the message is erotic doesn't mean the medium should be poorly executed. And just because the reader is indulging in sexual fantasy doesn't mean he'll settle for second-best. More to the point, neither will the editor. This is a professional business, and these days sex-book publishers require writers with professional skills.

This doesn't imply you need academic qualifications. Some of the most successful novelists I've met as an editor have had none to speak of. I was at a sales meeting once to which the publisher had invited its most successful fiction authors. They were an ill-assorted bunch, none of them young or glamorous or outwardly imposing. I doubt if they had more than a couple of O-levels between them – certainly none of them were university graduates. Yet they all spoke with passion and sincerity about their books in language that was simple yet effective. They knew, probably by instinct, how to tell a good story. And they sold books in enviable quantities.

That story-telling instinct is necessary for all novelists, in erotica as in every other category. I doubt if it can be learnt but it can probably be unlocked – certainly it can be polished and focused. I hope what follows will help you to focus your particular story-telling talents in this genre.

Respecting the reader

I can only hazard a guess at your motives for wanting to write an erotic novel, as opposed to any other kind. But if it is purely cynical, I'd advise you to think again. It may be that you've noticed a proliferation of sexy books on the shelves and concluded that 'there must be a market for this sort of thing.' Possibly you've read one or two and come to the conclusion that you could do it much better (and maybe you can). Now you're thinking, 'I'll dash one off and make some money while I plan my Booker Prize contender.' If that's the case, you might be in for an unwelcome surprise.

I used to meet aspiring authors who said they were going to knock out a Mills & Boon romance in their spare time. These were always young women whose bookshelves were stuffed with Virginia Woolf, Doris Lessing and the entire Virago backlist. They did not read Mills & Boon novels themselves but made the assumption that the task would be easy, that women's romances were simple fare and that their refined literary sensibilities would see them through without breaking sweat. Naturally, they failed. They did not respect the reader.

Nowadays, I suspect that everyone knows how difficult it is to write successfully for the women's romance market. The readers of Mills & Boon have very precise requirements and they can spot a phoney a mile off. Unless you share the dream they seek, you cannot invent one. You wouldn't write a science fiction novel or a detective story unless you liked reading those genres, would you? The same is true of erotic fiction.

The first thing you must do if you harbour feelings of patronage towards erotica is to read widely in the genre. Spend some time in a bookshop and flash the credit card (but keep the receipt – it's tax-deductible against your literary earnings). Read around the imprints, pay special attention to the covers and blurbs, try to find authors who particularly appeal to you. If what you discover leaves you cold then the money you've invested is still worth it – you now know you needn't waste your time.

Naturally this advice – read erotic novels – applies to all who wish to write one. One of the charms of the genre is the diversity of style and setting. This is of great importance to writers. Provided the book excites the reader, the writer is free to express himself in a multitude of ways. He or she can set it a thousand years in the past or a thousand in the future, borrow the clothing of a Gothic romance or a fairytale, and write it like Raymond Chandler or Jane Austen (true enough, try the novels of Louisa Campion). Compared to the territorial restrictions of most genres, the erotic writer can roam where he or she pleases.

Researching the market

So who is this reader you must respect? Publishers are notorious for not knowing their readers. It's not an area that is easy to research – even if it were affordable or desirable. Books are not like washing powder. Publishing is a small-margin, small-beer industry in comparison to many others. Publishers are not in the position to commission market research on their offerings. If there's any money available it is usually better spent elsewhere. Besides, how do you go about it? Novels, in particular, are irritatingly imprecise in their appeal.

That doesn't mean that publishers don't try. Headline have been running a back-of-the-book survey in their Delta imprint in an attempt to learn more about their readers. Here are some of the findings. You should know that respondents were lured with the promise of a free book (if they lived in the United Kingdom) and that Delta is aimed primarily at middle-of-the-road male heterosexual tastes.

The readership breaks down as follows:

Male respondents	73%	
Female	27%	
Age range	% age of readers	% of age group who are female
Under 20	3%	(60%)
20–30	24%	(47%)
30–40	23%	(35%)
40–50	26%	(15%)
50–60	13%	(8%)
60–70	8%	(0%)
Over 70	3%	(0%)

The overwhelming majority are regular book-buyers and readers in general. The most frequently cited non-erotic novelists read by this group are Stephen King, Terry Pratchett and Jackie Collins, closely followed by Tom Clancy, Wilbur Smith and Dick Francis. Respondents' tastes cover the literary landscape from Tom Sharpe to John Irving, from Danielle Steel to Gabriel García Márquez. The most frequently mentioned (British) newspaper is the *Sun*, with the *Daily Telegraph* and *Daily Mail* equal second, followed by *The Times*, the *Daily Express* and the *Daily Mirror*.

You may be a shrewder reader of the runes than me but I doubt if this tells you much (though the relatively high proportion of young women readers for a 'male' list is interesting). Canvas any bunch of unpretentious readers and you'd probably come up with similar populist results, bearing in mind the UK bias.

So how does this help you to write your erotic novel? It doesn't. It seems the average reader is a regular book-buyer, with wide-ranging if mainstream tastes, probably aged between twenty and fifty. This is not an easily identifiable sector of the population. There's nothing special about these people, except that they like reading sexy stories – just like you and me. Put it another way, for practical purposes the most important reader of your work is you. And when writing your novel you are the first person you must satisfy.

'Unless I am writing something that is good fun *for me*, not for somebody else, I cannot write at all.'

Arthur Ransome

Reading list

If you are interested in the history of pornographic publishing, look out for:

The Horn Book, G. Legman (1964)

The Other Victorians, Steven Marcus (1966)

The Secret Record, Michael Perkins (1976)

A History of Erotic Literature, Patrick J. Kearney (1982)

Key works of erotic literature

This is a small selection of well-known 'obscene' books whose unique voices have survived the disapproval of previous ages. Needless to say, their influence extends far beyond the erotic genre itself.

Memoirs of a Woman of Pleasure or *Fanny Hill*, John Cleland (1748)

Justine, Marquis de Sade (1791)

My Secret Life, 'Walter' (c.1890)

Lady Chatterley's Lover, D. H. Lawrence (1928)

Tropic of Cancer, Henry Miller (1934)

Delta of Venus, Anaïs Nin (1940/1, published 1969)

The Story of O, Pauline Réage (1954)

2
EROTIC STORY-TELLING

'The best erotic work is surely going to be very boring and repetitive without a good story to hang it on.'

Respondent to erotic survey

Getting going

The hoariest words of wisdom regularly offered to the would-be novelist are: write what you know. This is sound advice. It would be courting disaster to embark on a piece of fiction set in a nuclear reactor or a Swiss bank or even a local-government office if you had no idea how these environments functioned. Of course, you could find out and it's surprising how far a few nuggets of solid information can be made to stretch by a skilful writer.

As an erotic novelist, you are at an advantage over authors whose work requires in-depth knowledge of Sanskrit, keyhole surgery or what Henry VIII ate for breakfast. Unless you have been very unfortunate in life to date, you will have experienced erotic pleasures firsthand and forged sexual relationships – whether short or long-term doesn't matter. If you want to write a sexy novel, the chances are you have swum in the ocean of sexual experience and know what it's about. And if you've only got your toes wet, there are places to further your research and still stay dry – a trip to a bookshop and a video store will probably give you all the background you need.

We can assume then that you are equipped with the basic knowhow and are keen to forge ahead. Surely now it's just a question of boy takes girl back to his place and they work their way through the *Kama Sutra*? Hardly. Unless you are something of a genius in this sphere, confining yourself to two characters in one setting for an entire novel will soon bore you and your readers to tears. What you need is a plot.

What's the point of plotting an erotic novel?

Many people will be puzzled if you tell them you are working on a plot for an erotic novel. Maybe you yourself have doubts. As you struggle to come up with an original scenario a voice in your head or, quite likely, a friend or a partner will say, 'Why bother? Those books are all the same – just one bonk after another.' Then you'll wonder if you're wasting your time. Believe me, you're not.

The plot is the reason those bonks take place, the link that leads the reader on a journey from page one to page 256. And in taking that journey, if you do your job properly, readers will be thrilled, diverted and entertained just as they would be in reading any other kind of novel. They will also have engaged their sexual imagination – which is the point of this kind of book.

Just one carnal encounter after another is not a plot. It's not very interesting either for 70,000 plus words. One hot sex scene may make a vivid short story but a dozen in a row do not comprise a novel. If your reader simply wanted the thrill of men and women 'doing it', then a film would offer a better bet. Blue movies and videos are not renowned for their deft story lines or intriguing characters but they do provide unlimited footage of people 'doing it'.

Readers of erotic novels, however, want more than mere exposure to sexual activity. They want to be led into a fictional world in which people interact carnally within a dramatic framework. In other words, they want the kind of experience they get from a good read in other categories of fiction – and they want a vicarious sex thrill too. You, the novelist, must create this world and you won't be able to do it by keeping your characters in bed, serially copulating. You need a peg on which to hang the action, a reason for your characters being in a sexual frenzy, a dramatic framework that gives a point to the poking. Therefore, you need a plot.

What is an erotic plot?

There are many valuable guides to the art of fiction that offer insights into plot construction. Many quote E. M. Forster's famous definition of a plot and so will I. Given the nature of this particular book, I've taken a few liberties: 'The King fucked the chambermaid and the Queen fucked the footman' is an erotic story. 'The King fucked the chambermaid and the Queen fucked the footman for revenge' is an erotic plot.

In other words, a plot is more than a mere recitation of unconnected events, it's an interlocking sequence of cause and effect. It will strengthen your erotic novel considerably if there's a reason beyond physical attraction for your lovers to be embracing.

What makes a successful erotic plot?

The answer is: all the elements that make up effective fiction of any kind, plus sex. Here are some examples of erotic plots:

> Avelino, a young Spanish peasant, is stunned to discover a naked woman sunbathing on the beach. They make love and Janice, a visitor to his small village, is captivated by his innocence. He accepts her offer to leave his simple life and go to Barcelona to live with her. But the immorality of the city appals him. Janice proves to be unfaithful and her friends treat him as an available gigolo. When he discovers his lover is living off the proceeds of brothels that exploit under-age girls, he decides to inform the authorities. Before he can do so, hired killers come for him. He flees the city only to be shot at in the mountains and his car plunges over a ravine. He wakes to find his broken bones being tended by a band of gypsies, among

them a beautiful young girl who nurses him back to health and becomes his new lover. He doubts that he will ever return to the city.

With Open Mouth, Marcus Van Heller (1956)

Diana waits in a hotel bar for her husband who, as usual, is late. These days Charles pays her no attention and no longer makes love to her. She is so angry that, when an attractive stranger mistakes her for an escort girl, she goes up to his room. Half an hour later she's enjoyed the best sex she's had for years and is £150 better off. When the stranger calls she agrees to meet him again. It's not the money she craves, it's the erotic excitement. She entertains the stranger's friends, too. Suddenly, after years of abstinence, she's become voraciously sexual and she loves it. She signs on at an upmarket escort agency, planning to save enough money to divorce Charles. On a double date with a black prostitute who specialises in domination, she whips a blindfolded man who revels in her treatment – the man is Charles. Now she knows why her husband has neglected her for so long. In the last scene of the novel she confronts him: he can leave now or obey her every whim. As he sinks to his knees, it appears there may be life in her marriage after all...

Amateur Nights, Becky Bell (1993)

Kate is a naive English rose with a vivid fantasy life. Her marriage to the profligate Roger leaves her unsatisfied and – she suddenly discovers – on the brink of ruin. Roger's dissolute behaviour has placed her inheritance and home in jeopardy, and her fate now lies in the hands of DeVille, a purveyor of women to the wealthy. DeVille offers Kate a chance to redeem the debt – if she will become his sexual plaything for two weeks. Kate has no choice but to accept and is plunged into a whirl of sexual adventure with a variety of men and women that provides her with a comprehensive erotic education. In the end, having formed a close bond with a girl who has undergone a similar rite of passage, she avoids penury and emerges from her experience a satisfied woman in charge of her sensual destiny.

Two Weeks in May, Maria Caprio (1993)

Though inherently sexual, these plots all conform to the basic rules of the story-teller's art. We are introduced to a main character whose life is suddenly affected by an external event – the peasant's seduction by the city sophisticate, the wife's impulsive infidelity at the hotel, Kate's discovery that she stands on the brink of ruin. Like stones falling into a quiet pool, the consequences ripple through their lives as they face up to their new challenges. Avelino leaves his home to live with his new lover, the wife decides to become an amateur prostitute, Kate agrees to become a sexual slave for two weeks. The middle section of each book recounts how the protagonist deals with these new circumstances – there are set-backs to which they must respond, usually with the help of key secondary characters who act as guides on the journey. Eventually, at the end of each book, the situation is resolved as the hero or heroine completes his quest and discovers that he or she now possesses a greater measure of self-knowledge.

In brief, an effective erotic plot requires a character whom readers care about facing up to a challenge, preferably in an intriguing setting. And, since this is erotica, that challenge must be of a sexual nature. Though we've all read erotic novels in which the sexual episodes have been grafted on to a conventional plot, the best of them place erotic events and relationships at the heart of the tale. It is wise not to assume that by adding a few thousand words of sensual description to your rejected spy story you will arrive at a publishable erotic novel. Quite possibly you can adapt that idea successfully to the genre but you'll need to rework it substantially so that the sexual element is integral and not mere decoration.

That said, the distinguishing nature of the erotic genre is the evocative description of sexual events and the plot you devise must be sufficiently adaptable to provide those moments. In which case, it helps to be aware of certain factors particular to the construction of erotic novels. For ease of reference, I call these The Blue Rules and your plot should take them into account.

The Blue Rules

1. The plot must provide opportunities for frequent sexual activity

Exactly how much sex is required in this kind of novel will vary from publisher to publisher – in any event such things are hard to quantify. A basic guideline is to assume that you must provide at least one major erotic scene in every chapter. Assuming a chapter length of four or five thousand words, that means fifteen to twenty significant encounters in the whole novel. Another common way of looking at it suggests that about half the action of your book should be sexual, with your characters either engaged in sexual activity or fore-and-after play.

Given that, your scenario must have sexual potential. The adventures of a shipwreck survivor on a deserted island, a lone round-the-world-yachtsman or an astronaut on a solo trip to Mars do not provide obvious opportunities for the erotic novelist.

Not that it can't be done. Kitt Gerrard's *Midnight Tales of Torment* is set almost entirely in an Antarctic listening-post manned by two intelligence agents – a man and a woman – whose professional integrity forbids them from entering into a physical relationship. As their frustration gets the better of them, they agree to tell each other erotic bedtime stories, with the result that the novel is inhabited by a cast of characters drawn from reminiscence, fantasy and tales-within-tales. You may find it easier – though distinctly less original – to make your hero a travelling salesman.

2. The plot should concern sexually active adults

The fact is, your characters, for whatever reason, have to have sex – lots of it. Your heroine may begin the book as a dry-as-dust bluestocking but by the end she will have frolicked naked beneath the stars in the grip of erotic ecstasy beyond her wildest dreams – and we will have lived every moment of the experience with her. So, stories built round dedicated virgins and celibates with no interest in sexual activity won't work. Restrict non-participants to walk-on parts. These books allow no spectators – except for dedicated voyeurs whose presence is tolerated because the reader is allowed, usually by way of variety, to look through their eyes.

Occasionally a non-participant can provide a counterpoint to the activities of the novel – in which case he or she must play a significant role in the plot. The celibacy of such characters rarely endures to the end of the novel for obvious reasons. Given the prevailing atmosphere, no one's will-power is that strong.

> She came close, her breasts undulating inches from his face. Inspector Monk couldn't help himself. Fifteen years of abstinence had not wiped from his memory the ecstasies of the flesh. As he touched her, those fifteen barren years might never have been.
>
> *Lust at Large*, Noel Amos (1994)

3. The plot should offer erotic variety

One of the challenges in writing an erotic novel is to avoid boring the reader. Beware of repetition. If the first half a dozen sex scenes in your book are of the same lovers in the same bed having missionary-position sex then your reader will feel cheated – and you'll be yawning your head off. In the world of fantasy fucking that your book creates for the reader, each encounter must be special in its own way. The simplest method of doing this is to ring the changes. That means providing variety of setting, activity and – probably most important – personnel.

Erotic novels offer readers the promise of a sexual freedom they do not enjoy in real life. The point of them, for many people, is that they give the reader a choice of (imaginary) sexual partners. And though it would be possible to write a book about an entirely monogamous relationship, a cast of diverse characters will be more satisfying to write and read about.

On a practical level, a variety of characters casts your net wider. Look at hit TV shows such as *Dallas*, *Thirtysomething*, *LA Law* and *Friends*. These are slick and skilful entertainments but an element of their success is surely that they are packed with many different attractive performers. As a friend said to me when *Dallas* was first broadcast, 'It can't fail. There's someone in it for everyone to fancy.' It's useful to bear that in mind when constructing your plot. Resist making all the women twenty-year-old blondes with jobs in public relations and the men designer-jeaned photographers with long lenses. These particular fantasy models may light your fire but you'll bore most readers by Chapter 5.

The Blue Rules at work

Here's a (very unoriginal) idea for a detective novel. A private detective is hired to track down some stolen papers. His investigation leads him to a number of suspicious characters and he has to exert all his skills to extract the information he needs that will lead him to the next contact in the chain. In the end, and after a suitably tense finale, he completes his quest.

Apply the Blue Rules and the idea becomes much more interesting. Suppose the missing papers have an erotic significance: a salacious correspondence between a politician and his mistress or incriminating photos of marital infidelity or – best of all – the sex diary of the aloof and beautiful film star who hires the detective in the first place. Of course, the suspicious characters the private eye encounters turn out to be women of different types and he uses a variety of techniques to winkle what he wants out of them. To succeed, he must confront his own sexual nature, submitting to bondage, accompanying an informer to a fetish club, participating in group sex – there are many possibilities. Finally he returns triumphant to his seductive employer to claim the special bonus she promised him if he succeeded – her body. The last page finds him exhausted but satisfied – it's a dirty job but someone's got to do it. We could call the novel *Mean Sheets*...

This is a bit of a joke but it makes a point. Here there are numerous opportunities for erotic scenes that, because of the inherently sexual nature of the plot, won't slow down the narrative. Every character in the book is erotically involved and there's no limit to the number of people our hero can tussle with. And, by adopting the point-of-view of the protagonist as he puts his sexuality on the line to crack the case, the author can take the reader on a thrilling journey of ever-increasing erotic excitement.

It is worth noting that the detective, though no virgin at the beginning, should have had strictly conventional sexual experiences so that, in the course of the book, he is forced to become a little more reckless. And – guess what – he likes the change of pace. On reflection, I'd make the detective a woman and reverse most (but not all) of the other sexual polarities. Then we'd have a young feisty female in the hot seat, refusing to flinch from a succession of sexual challenges. This would make the whole private-eye scenario less old-fashioned, more V. I. Warshawski than Philip Marlowe. It would also strengthen the notion of an uninitiated protagonist who comes to embrace the delights of uninhibited sexuality – a common character progression in erotica.

Whether this book would be any good would depend on many other factors – whether the characters are inventively drawn, whether the author can avoid the obvious clichés, above all whether the sex scenes can fire up the reader. The structure, however, is both sound enough and flexible enough to work.

Outlines

An outline is a précis of the plot of your novel. It can be as short as half a page – a mere summation of an idea – or it can be a detailed chapter-by-chapter breakdown running to a dozen or more pages.

'All artists plan their work. Painters make sketches, sculptors make models, composers write drafts, actors rehearse. Authors write outlines.'

Celia Brayfield, *Bestseller* (1996)

An alternative school of thought decrees that no planning is necessary, that a writer can take an opening situation and let it roll until he hits his target word count. Known in some circles as the Narrative Push method, this form of working claims the advantage of spontaneity. I suspect that this is the same kind of spontaneity that prevents a writer revising his work on the grounds that first thoughts are always the best (I've had this excuse). In other words, the author is trying to cut corners. You might be able to pull it off in this genre if you're an experienced operator – especially if your sexy scenes are sufficiently exciting – but I wouldn't recommend it for the beginner. This is the kind of high-wire act that often leaves the practitioner on the ground and 50,000 words in the bin.

In fact the experienced professionals all plan their work to some degree. I recently canvassed the opinions of a dozen or so authors, all with many published titles to their credit, and every one of them writes outlines in one form or another. Some restrict themselves to a simple one-page summary, others produce a short plan and then a detailed chapter breakdown. These pages are used to solicit commissions from publishers but there are other reasons for producing them. Authors write plot plans to give themselves confidence that the idea will work as a novel. Though short, these summaries are often quite sophisticated. From them an experienced author will be able to judge the shape of the finished book and ensure that the plot will fulfil the publisher's required word count.

The received wisdom for the beginner is: write an outline even if you don't like it. Something on paper is always better than nothing. And if you don't like your plan then you'll know what to avoid when you write your next one – which, if you are serious about writing erotica, will be very soon.

Your turn

Why don't you, just for fun, see if you can come up with a short outline for an erotic novel? Half a page will do but it can't just be a recitation of events, the action must be causal – remember E. M. Forster. It must also be more than an opening situation. Ideally it should have a beginning, a middle and an end – and, as erotic writer Valentina Cilescu puts it, 'a feeling'.

Here's some ideas to start you off.

Pick one of the following movies:

Annie Hall
Cabaret
Casablanca
Chinatown
The English Patient.

Try and convert the plot into an erotic scenario using the Blue Rules. It's not as mad an idea as you may think.

If you aren't familiar with any of the above (where have you been?) try the same exercise based on a film you do know. Note that you need a relationship-based scenario – it won't work with *The Battleship Potemkin.*

3

LIBERATING THE IMAGINATION

> 'When in doubt, make a fool of yourself. There is a
> microscopically thin line between being brilliantly
> creative and acting like the most gigantic idiot on earth.
> So, what the hell, leap.'
>
> Cynthia Heimel

How do I get ideas?

Ideas – just one good one will do – are what you need before you can
plot your novel. You also need specific erotic ideas for all those
significant sex scenes that the genre requires. Unfortunately, there is
no guaranteed source labelled Ideas for Erotic Novelists – not that it
would do you much good. A stimulating idea for one writer is hopeless
for the next. You must find your own sources, those that speak directly
to you. I have no doubt they lie within you right now – in your dreams,
your memories, in the dark silt of your unconscious. Sometimes it
helps to stir the silt and send a bubble floating to the surface, into the
daylight where you can recognise it for the gem it is. And sometimes
it is necessary to kick-start the creative process. Erotic novel-writing
is a professional business and nobody earns a penny waiting for the
muse to call.

I have asked several authors where they get their inspiration from.
Some are vague, a few are guarded, but most are keen to be helpful.
Here are some of the most useful replies:

'Films and newspapers.'

'Other novels – I sometimes take a character out of context and make him or her mine in a different situation.'

'Agony columns in magazines and lonely hearts ads.'

'Photographic journals or diaries – one good picture can spark me off.'

'Sometimes I find an interesting sub-plot in another novel and change it completely.'

'Things I've done.'

'Places. Also museums – I always take a notebook.'

'I get people drunk and steal their fantasies. Unfortunately my friends are wise to me now.'

All these ideas have possibilities and I offer them as examples of what works for others. You must discover what works for you.

On this topic, authors also say where ideas *don't* come from – namely other people. If you're a writer there's a good chance that one day someone will say, 'I've got this brilliant plot for a book. I don't have time to write it but why don't you?' When this happens be polite but don't get your hopes up. Though it may be a thrilling notion for your friend, the chances are it will not work for you. Writers must have a personal stake in the creation of a plot for the book to be their own. It rarely works for a writer to put on second-hand clothes – it's like donning a straitjacket. As an editor, though I can't resist having my two-penny-worth, I no longer give ready-made plots to authors because I've discovered they are not of any use to them.

This is not to say that writers shouldn't use other people's ideas as a jumping-off point – as in the comments above about adapting a character or sub-plot from another novel. If it's all right for Shakespeare to plunder the *Chronicles* of Holinshed, then it's accept-able for the rest of us and indeed is a time-honoured practice. If you are short of an idea for a plot you could do worse than begin with Shakespeare, whose story lines have been hijacked on a regular basis. An erotic *Romeo and Juliet*? A sexy *Othello* in which Desdemona really did do the deed with Cassio? Change the period, lighten the tone, alter the endings – this is not entirely a joke suggestion. There are no new stories, they say, only new ways to tell the old ones. (Note the information on copyright infringement that follows in Chapter 9.)

In all probability your ideas will just arrive in your head, the product of unconscious thought processes that you cannot analyse. Most of the writers I've quoted spoke of this phenomenon: 'there's a coming together of disparate ideas', 'it's just something in the air', 'on Friday evening I didn't have a clue but when I woke up on Saturday I knew just what to write'. You could say that's what makes these people writers and put it down to the magic of their innate creativity. On the other hand, you could recognise this ability in yourself.

All of us are faced with problems that don't, on the surface, look solvable and yet we come up with solutions. We arrange weddings and family celebrations, select birthday presents for people impossible to please, decorate rooms and apartments – these may seem mechanical tasks compared to creating a full-length work of fiction but they're fraught with pitfalls and require expert decision-making. In all of the domestic challenges of life we find solutions based to a greater or lesser extent on information we have gathered. We devote time to research, visualise the consequences of this choice or that, listen to our hearts and our heads – then we make a choice. Much of writing a novel involves the same thought processes.

If you've read erotic novels, accept the genre's unique mission to thrill, are aware of the Blue Rules and alert to the culture around you *and you still haven't got a clue what you are going to write*, I'll be surprised. You probably haven't asked yourself a crucial question.

What if?

What if you actually talked to the tall guy who says hello on your train every morning? What if you had gone skinny-dipping when the three of you were sloshed one night in France? What if you'd made a pass at Mrs Price when she'd asked you to cut her lawn that hot afternoon in your last term at college? Remember how she asked you in for a beer, looking good enough to eat in a tight bikini top and little white shorts...

I'm getting carried away, as you can see, but only to demonstrate the advantages of asking yourself 'what if?' This line of thinking is very useful to any novelist. Simple questions like 'what if?', 'suppose that?' and 'I wonder whether?' invariably get the writer's mind working. Then it's a question of running with the idea, testing one set of circumstances against another and seeing what develops.

This doesn't have to be done sitting at a desk or staring at a notepad. Playing make-believe, in my opinion, is most productive while engaged in some other task, preferably something familiar and humdrum that you can do in your sleep. Washing-up, ironing, walking the dog, working out at the gym – these are the kind of activities that part of your brain will deal with efficiently while you think about your book.

Internal brainstorming is second nature to most writers, and for the erotic writer no less than any other. If it worries you that you are dreaming of a hot date with a guy who looks like Mel Gibson while making the kids' supper, remember that you are also test-driving a scene from your novel. All over the world, men and women are using erotic fantasies to brighten their unremarkable lives – but, unlike you, they stand no chance of getting a publishing contract out of it.

Note-taking and other practicalities

The time to start writing is when you have conjured something up in your mind, not before. It is universally accepted that the most intimidating article a writer ever faces is a blank sheet of paper. In which case, it helps to approach that paper with an idea of what you are going to put on it.

There are no hard-and-fast rules about how to capture your inspiration on the page. The standard advice is always to carry pencil and paper, to have them by your bedside to record your dreams, and in your pocket when you're out walking the street, alive to snippets of overheard conversation from passers-by. I remember a writer who transcribed dinner-party *bon mots* on to cigarette packets while at the table, which is not a habit to be recommended if you want to remain popular – especially if you're writing erotica.

Notes, of course, need to be kept in order so you can find them when you want to. Together with the cuttings you've probably snipped from newspapers and magazines, the old photos from junk shops and jottings from trips to museums (if you follow the author's advice given above) you might have box loads of material cluttering up your kitchen table or bedroom or whatever passes for your writing area. Frankly, how you handle all this is up to you. Other books can advise you on how to organise and file your research material. Some of them will give you good ideas on what kind of chair to sit on and whether to use a pencil or a PC. I have every confidence you're clever enough to evolve your own method. Only two things are important:

1. Don't throw anything away till you've finished the book. If you do, you're bound to regret it.

2. Your finished work must be typed somehow. No publisher will read longhand script.

If, after a time, you are surrounded by chaos and feel you are getting nowhere, don't despair. Any information you can amass on your project will be useful, either directly or indirectly.

The Iceberg Theory

The Iceberg Theory holds that a novel is like an iceberg, only revealing a fifth of its bulk above the waves. That's what the reader sees. The author, however, must be aware of the hidden four-fifths that keeps the iceberg afloat.

In other words, you must know much more about your book than anybody else. And all those half-baked notions and dead-end irrelevancies cluttering up your desk are part of that knowledge.

'If a writer omits something because he does not know it, then there is a hole in the story.'

Ernest Hemingway

But, just as important, you don't need to show everything you know. For instance, apprentice novelists often feel they must account to the reader for every waking moment of their protagonist's time. They say, 'On Wednesday morning Jim got up late, had breakfast of toast and black coffee and read the paper till it was time to go round to Rosie's.' The reader doesn't need the domestic trivia. Unless there's a particular reason to describe the events of Jim's morning, leave it out. It's enough for you, the author, to know what your hero got up to. Don't bore the rest of us. Think cinema and cut straight to the orgy at Rosie's place.

Order out of chaos

At this stage you will probably want to reduce your book to a simple plan on one sheet of paper. There are some handy ways to do this, often recommended to new writers.

1. The linear method

Take a sheet of paper and number it down the left-hand side from one to fifteen. The numbers stand for a chapter, based on the assumption that there will be fifteen chapters of five thousand words in your book – a calculation of convenience only. Against each number – or as many as you can – write down the significant points in your plot. The chances are, you'll be able to fill in from 1 – 5 with ease, possibly 14 and 15 and have a vague stab at a couple of points in between. Don't fill in blanks for the sake of doing so. This isn't a crossword puzzle, it's the skeleton plan of your novel. And even if you're missing every bone from the sternum to the ankle it is still a useful exercise. You can tell at a glance how far your plan has progressed and where you must concentrate your thinking to complete it further.

2 The schematic method

This offers another way of looking at your book. On your blank sheet of paper write down the names of your main characters. If you have one leading character put that slap in the middle of your space; if there are two or three or more, spread them out. Around them place secondary characters and connect them with lines. The idea is to depict the linking relationships and the thrust of the action. You can also add character details – their principal traits, their goals, their physical characteristics. Similarly you can put notes on locations, atmosphere and other salient points. You can make this a simple five-minute exercise or a longer task – there is no limit to the size of paper you can use or the number of coloured pens. The idea is to take a fresh look at the balance of relationships and where the significant lines of action take place. The resulting chart can be most revealing, particularly in a novel with a lot of plot strands. And for the erotic novelist, keen for obvious reasons to exploit the physical relationships of his or her characters, it can reveal whole areas of missed opportunity.

There are other methods but they basically fall into these two categories, linear and schematic. The most valuable is a variation on the first in which you write the significant steps of your plot on cards so you can then shuffle the order and see how things look in a different sequence.

It's important to remember that the pieces of paper you produce in this way are just working documents, exercises that may or may not be of value to you. You may consider them a waste of time but until you've tried them out you won't know. They are also not mutually exclusive. Sometimes it's valuable to subject your work-in-progress to both kinds of scrutiny – especially if you're stuck. The idea is that once you get the bones of the plot down then you can decide the best way of telling the tale.

Your turn

Two teenagers from opposing backgrounds fall passionately in love. Their families are bitterly against the attachment and the girl's father arranges for her to be sent to school in another country. They run away a day before her plane leaves and the families pursue them. The lovers have twenty-four hours to decide whether to give up or escape for good – and to slake each other's physical need. Think *Romeo and Juliet* and try and work the scenario into an erotic plot. If the idea appeals, give the warring families personalities in your mind (for example, maybe not all of them are in opposition); try out various settings and periods; examine the reasons for the antagonism; develop further erotic connections between the cast of characters.

Look through some recent newspapers or magazines. See if you can find a story that has erotic possibilities. Women's magazines such as *Marie Claire* and *Cosmopolitan* are particularly fruitful. They are packed with fascinating interview-based stories under headings such as 'Too Damned Beautiful: Women who are too pretty to have successful relationships' and 'Sexual Surprises: Real tales of unexpected pleasure'.

If you have an idea of your own, see how it translates into the linear and schematic methods described above.

'Cast' your idea with film and TV actors who attract you. (If this doesn't get your erotic fantasies in gear you're in the wrong genre.)

If you have no notion yet what you may write, take a book you know well and see how that can be reduced to a diagram.

4
SEXY STRUCTURE

> 'As in all my books for a long time the problem was structure. I never start writing until I've sorted that out.'
>
> Gabriel García Márquez

The shape of your novel

An erotic novel advances in peaks and troughs, with the peaks representing significant sexual moments in the plot. The book should start with a grabby opening that hooks the reader into the story and indicates the level of erotic stimulation to follow. Then the narrative can be established in a less fevered manner before moving on to the next sex scene and then the next. Naturally, these scenes should be varied – in deed or location or personnel – and the pitch of excitement should ascend, as if you are building a stairway and each erotic moment is a step, until you reach the figurative and literal climax of the novel. Ideally, the plot should walk hand-in-hand with this upward progression until it too is resolved.

Notwithstanding the need for a seductive opening, most writers would not begin their novel with a ten-page orgy – they would save it for the end of the novel. Similarly they would not finish with a tender, two-person love scene unless as a postscript to the wild hedonism of the culmination of events.

First moves

'I'll tell you a secret – *nobody* knows how to start a novel.
There are no rules, because each novel is a case unto itself.'

Lawrence Block, *Telling Lies for Fun and Profit* (1981)

'The last thing one discovers in writing a book is what to put first.'

Blaise Pascal

The first few paragraphs of your novel are likely to be the most important you will write. These are the lines an editor reads first and, probably, the ones a casual browser in a bookshop will look at once he has picked up the book. Bear in mind it would be just as easy for him to put it down again. The browser will first have been attracted by the illustration on the front cover, then have his interest captured by the copy on the back. His expectations of an arousing read are high as he then turns to page one of the narrative. Now's your chance to hook your fish. Do you plunge straight into an episode of startling frankness or do you set the scene and make him wait?

I'm sure you know the answer to this already. If you begin your novel with a sentence such as: '*"Fuck me now," moaned the big-breasted blonde as she grasped Luc's swollen cock in her fist*' then you risk turning as many readers off as on. Even those to whom recognised turn-on terms (see Chapter 6) such as '*fuck me now*', '*big-breasted*' and '*swollen cock*' have appeal are unlikely to respond to having them thrown in their faces in the first line.

As a rule, it is preferable to place your reader in a specific situation – usually a titillating one – that enables him or her to get acquainted with your characters before hitting the ecstasy button. Like the first sight of a desirable stranger, the promise of erotic pleasure should be tangible though the realisation is still to come. At the same time, there are a lot of other things for a writer to do at this point – not least informing the reader what's going on in a clear and sympathetic voice.

Here are some sample beginnings.

> Lean cheeks hot, heart pounding, Avelino the singer heaved himself quietly up the last two centimetres of rock to look down on the naked unsuspecting woman below.
>
> The noise of a dislodged stone as he settled himself in a niche was drowned by the washing of the surf close to the woman's prostrate body. He gazed at her with the frightened, formless anguish of his twenty-one sexless years and it was as if cold sea-water had suddenly swamped his loins.
>
> *With Open Mouth*, Marcus Van Heller (1956)

Here we have a precise picture of the young voyeur on the cliff looking down at the woman on the beach. She's naked, he's excited, they're going to get together – but how? Before he can make the approach which we, the readers, anticipate will end in an act of passionate love-making, he must conquer the fear that goes with his virginity. This fear – 'the frightened, formless anguish of his twenty-one sexless years' – turns him from a possible predator, a threat to the woman below, into a person who attracts our sympathy. We want to know what happens to him next.

> The moon hung round and white as a buxom maiden's breast over the stable. A gentle breeze rustled through tall pines and cypresses standing about the building like dark sentinels.
>
> Within were a man and a maid, playing the ancient game of love – though between these two the term was lust, not love. The man was red of hair and brawny of build and his big body covered hers fully. She writhed in pleasure, a sun-bronzed country girl who was still partially clothed. Her moans rose along with sighs and gasps, accompanied by the sound of hay rustling beneath her.

> Neither of them knew that they were being watched.
>
> *The Crusader*, John Cleve (1974)

The opening image – the breast-like moon – could be deemed corny but it works and it puts a sensuous image directly into the reader's head in the first line. Even as the author sets the scene – the night, the stable, the wind in the trees – he's established an erotic atmosphere. Like a film-maker, the author pans in from the landscape to the interior of the stable where a man and a woman are embracing on the rustling hay. Then he tells us they are being watched. If the browser is not intrigued by the scenario at this point then he's unlikely ever to be.

> When I was twenty-three I saw Jean Genet's notorious play, *The Balcony*, the story of a brothel where men act out their fantasies of power and cruelty among submissive whores and mirrors. This was in California on a sweltering hot night. The men in the audience took off their jackets, ran with sweat and looked at their female companions with predatory eyes. I found myself recoiling from the prospect of the savage, imitative fantasies which would be acted out that night in the decorous suburbs of Santa Barbara. And as I left the theater I was seized by a perverse obsession which has not released me from that day to this: to find, somewhere in the world, the obverse of Genet's dream. A whorehouse where women force their fantasies on the visiting men, creating the wildest rigmaroles and scenarios in their craving for satisfaction. Would men pay to enter such a place? I know *I* would.
>
> *Dreams of Fair Women*, Celeste Arden (1987)

Here's a different kettle of fish, related in the first person. Though the author puts us in a specific time and place – a sweltering theatre where excited men devour the women with their eyes – the narrator is selling us an idea. What's more, this idea is a distinctly intellectual concept, based on a play by Jean Genet. This is a bold and difficult way to open an erotic novel. Yet, to my mind, it is worth it. Once we have understood the phrase 'the obverse of Genet's dream' – which is explained in the next sentence – then we have bought the concept of the whole book, which is a quest to discover a whorehouse where *women's* fantasies are revealed to men.

> Matt found the magazine on his desk when he came back from lunch. There was a note from his partner pinned to it.
>
> He couldn't believe it at first – he thought the woman must be some lookalike – but closer inspection showed that it was in fact their living room she'd been photographed in and their sofa she was lying on with her legs wide apart and her vulva on full display.
>
> She was one of several readers' wives featured that month, but the only one who happened to be married to him.
>
> *Room Service*, Felice Ash (1996)

This is a shock opening, a mini-drama of suspense complete with punch-line. We picture the man at the desk looking at the magazine, taking in the obscene photograph, trying to resist the evidence before his eyes that the woman with her legs spread on his sofa is his wife. What happens next? I bet you want to know. The reader's attention has been engaged in under a hundred words.

In each of these beginnings – and I'm resisting quoting any more – the writer has captured the reader's interest by:

1. Painting a precise word picture
2. Making it clear that the forthcoming drama will feature sexual behaviour
3. Pointing the reader down the path the novel is to take.

If we want to have our expectations of erotic excitement fulfilled, we have to follow the author down that path.

Do I need a sub-plot?

'We are an audience trained by visual media, by television, film and commercials, an audience which is perfectly comfortable with thirty-five concurrent plot lines and near-subliminal images. In fact, we love all that.'

Celia Brayfield, *Bestseller* (1996)

Many erotic novels run from A to B to C in a straight line with not a sub-plot or a flashback in sight. This is absolutely fine if that is how you wish to proceed. A straightforward narrative with a beginning and a middle and an end is an excellent way to tell any story. If the pudding is good, why over-egg it? But you *can* follow a different recipe if you want to. Though I'm not advocating technical innovation on the scale of the experimental novelist, erotic writers are allowed to stretch their wings. Sometimes there are good reasons for doing so.

There are many erotic novels that do not follow their protagonist from first page to last but which switch between two or more narrative strands – though you can't do this if you have chosen to write in the first person (two first-person narratives in one book usually leads to confusion). *Your Cheating Heart* by Tom Crewe and Amber Wells, for example, interleaves the adventures of Sherrylee and Vinnie, a feckless married couple who spend most of their time coupling in any bed but the marital one. *Three Women* by Jocelyn Joyce goes a step further and entwines the separate *amours* of the three women of the title. The Lust novels by Noel Amos juggle several plot lines at a time, cutting backwards and forwards in short takes. *The Sex Files* series, four books by different authors using common characters, follows the investigations of the two protagonists while incorporating newspaper cuttings, wire-tap transcripts and vignettes of minor characters to ape the shape of a fast-paced TV thriller.

There are several advantages in moving the focus of the action. Providing variety (Blue Rule 3) is one. If your plot demands that A beds B twice in quick succession, it makes sense to cut away between these events to advance the affair between X and Y. And if this makes life more interesting for the reader, the same follows for the writer. The last emotion you want to feel when writing a passage of rousing excitement is boredom – it soon communicates itself to the reader.

Apart from variety, switching to a sub-plot can also change the pace. If your main plot is basically a mystery, by cutting in and out at the right moment you can build cliff-hangers into the action and heighten suspense. This kind of technique is used to effect in other genres – thrillers and crime fiction, obviously – but there's no reason why it can't be used in erotica.

There's only one over-riding condition – your novel must be sexy enough. If it fulfils that criteria the author can proceed how he or she likes.

Flashbacks

I have a personal preference for novels with a strong forward momentum. 'Don't look back' seems to me a good motto for a novelist. However, there are times when the story must shift back in time so that the rest of the book can go forward. Think of the flashback in *Casablanca* – the Paris scenes. Only after we've experienced that short sequence of the happy lovers before the outbreak of war, and understood the depth of feeling they have for each other, can the movie stride towards its poignant conclusion. Without it, the drama of Rick and Ilse's predicament would mean little.

In erotica, too, there are books that depend on the flashback for their full effect. The hero of Noel Amos's *Lust Under Licence* is a thrusting business mogul, Tom Glass, who has lost his memory after being pushed off his tenth-floor penthouse balcony. Under pressure from the jackbooted mistresses of the Sex Police, who wish to place Glass on trial, his doctor administers drugs that bring his life back to him in a series of erotic flashbacks. The novel comprises a present-day narrative in which a variety of women, none of whom he can recall, visit him in his tumescent convalescence and a back story made up of sexy snapshots from his past. Finally the two narratives combine and we find out which of the women in his life caused his tumble from the balcony.

The Diana Saxon novels of Lesley Asquith – *Sex and Mrs Saxon, Sin and Mrs Saxon* and *Lust and Lady Saxon* – also make free use of the flashback, to the extent that each book is split into two separate story lines, some twenty-odd years apart. Both narratives are related by the heroine (which contradicts my contention above that two first-person narratives in one novel don't work – though this *is* the same narrator). The result is effective, as we switch back and forth in the life of one woman, and certainly a neat variation on the played-out autobiographical form that has dominated much erotic writing of previous eras.

The problem with flashbacks is that they can unbalance the whole book and if there are too many the reader may be irritated at having to constantly readjust. If you find your flashback sequences taking over your novel, ask yourself whether you shouldn't be writing two separate stories. And, tempting though it is to throw in a character's carnal reminiscence to cover up the fact that there's no sexy action going on in your main storyline, you should use the device sparingly. Remember, the real test of a flashback is: does it carry the book forward?

Locations

The advantage of working in any genre is that you know – broadly speaking – what you will be writing about and who some of the personnel will be. If it's a crime novel there will be a violation of the law and it's likely the cast will contain police and detectives, even if only amateur ones. A legal thriller requires lawyers, their clients and the courtroom; a medical drama demands doctors and hospitals. And so on. But an erotic novel is about sex and has no preordained field of action or roster of characters. Lecherous minds and attractive bodies – which *are* a requirement of the genre – are not confined to any particular sphere of activity.

One of the erotic novelist's tricks is to create a separate ambience in which conventional morals and inhibitions can be set aside. Hence the prevalence of settings that are, in themselves, self-enclosed, where the reader can easily suspend disbelief. In self-contained worlds such as the harem, the whorehouse, the finishing school, it is possible to believe that anything goes. This impression can sometimes be heightened by setting the action back in time: the sea-crossing on a 1920s' ocean liner, for example, or a Victorian country-house party or the court of a Roman emperor.

Editors like new locations. By definition, they are fully acquainted with the familiar ones – exotic islands, coastal resorts of the rich and famous, hotels, health clubs, sex clubs, the sets of blue movies. Similarly, the worlds of advertising, television, cinema, music, art, fashion, journalism – you name any profession at all glamorous – have been used as backgrounds for these books. Which doesn't mean you can't use them, but do try and avoid the obvious clichés.

Period novels

If you like historical fiction and have an interest in a particular period this might well provide a suitable background for your novel. Women's erotica of recent years has injected new life into little-known ages of history (see Chapter 8). There has been so much Victorian and Edwardian material, some of it genuine and much of it ersatz, that you may be well advised to steer clear of the nineteenth- and early twentieth-century, but this still leaves you plenty of scope.

A period setting has evident advantages and disadvantages. You have to trust that the glimpse of an unknown world that your surroundings provide will attract more readers than those it repels. If you place your erotic drama in Egypt, say, at the court of Tutankhamun, it may well catch the fancy of those who like exotic detail in their titillating reading. On the other hand, some people will be put off by the difficult names and find it hard to identify with men and women who lived more than three thousand years ago.

You should also consider the extra work that such a project will entail. If you are already steeped in a period and it inspires your sensual imagination then this may be the route for you. If you have to undertake a lot of research before you can embark on the project with confidence then you must ask yourself if you can afford the time. It may be that you should be directing your efforts at a broader market. For most of us, there would be little point in spending years crafting a genre erotic novel.

The erotic imperative

No matter how rich the ambience of your novel or thrilling the period in which you have set it, don't lose sight of your main objective. The point of these books is to tell a sexy story. So, although it matters that the heroine solves the crime/gets the producer's job/becomes a film star and so on, the most important thing is that she gets laid – often and in explicit detail.

At the end of *Casablanca*, Rick says (famously), 'The problems of three little people don't amount to a hill of beans in this crazy world'. In terms of the audience in the cinema, this is baloney. The *only* thing that matters to them is what happens to Rick and Ilse. Sod the war, Bogie, get the girl.

The parallel with erotica – with any fiction – is obvious. Your characters are paramount in the eyes of the readers and it is their individual fate, not that of nations, that takes precedence. In the London Library I came across the reminiscences of a Frenchman who lived in Paris throughout the years of the Revolution. In his old age he was asked what it was like to live through the Terror. He said, 'I can't remember – I was in love at the time.' The fact is that history may march around us but sometimes we can see no farther than the lover by our side.

Location as character

Having stated something in categorical terms, it's as well to contradict it at once. There are novels in which the scenery is of greater significance than the actors on the stage. This is the case when the author seeks to create a large canvas, of a place (Edward Rutherfurd's *Sarum*, for example) or a time (Alexander Solzhenitsyn's *August 1914*) or even an industry (Arthur Hailey's *Wheels*). In these epics, the dramas of individuals are like jigsaw pieces that the author fits together to make a big picture.

The equivalent exists in erotica, though not on the scale of the novels mentioned above. Jocelyn Joyce's *Hotel D'Amour*, for example, uses a hotel in the French Alps as the connection between a variety of characters – a pair of American newly-weds who haven't yet hit it off in bed, a French adventuress aiming to snare a millionaire, an English lesbian and her latest flame, a Swedish couple who take up group sex, and so on. There is no plot beyond the place itself, which provides the link for a series of short sexy episodes. It's a simple device but effective. Similarly the Anne-Marie Villefranche novels – *Plaisir D'Amour*, *Joie D'Amour*, *Folies D'Amour* – are really themed collections of stories, in which characters appear and reappear at the author's whim, the sum of their experiences adding up to an erotic 'memoir' of Paris in the twenties. It's an approach that might appeal to you if you are nervous about deploying the same characters over 70,000 words, particularly if you are aware of publishers' frequently stated resistance to short story collections.

Endings

I'm a traditionalist when it comes to endings – loose plot strands should be tied up, the bad should have their bottoms smacked and the good should sail into a future of carnal bliss. In erotica, a climax means just that.

A question to pose yourself as you breast the finishing tape is: have I fulfilled all expectations? Or, to put it more directly, has everybody got laid? It is a crime in erotica to introduce an attractive character and not put him or her through their sexual paces – though this is an oversight easily perpetrated. For example, the novelist gives a hunky ski-instructor an early walk-on, intending to develop his slalom technique with the heroine at a later date. Unfortunately for the ski-instructor, the lady in question has her hands so full elsewhere that she never returns for her lesson and the novel finishes without keeping a promise to the reader. In this situation the novelist should revise, either by writing the instructor out or giving him his moment of glory on the slopes. Neglecting to fuck the fuckable, in this genre, is equivalent to placing a pistol on stage in a drama and not having it go off. The reader will close the book thinking, 'Whatever happened to Sven?' Don't get lazy, have Sven go pop like everyone else.

Erotica is not as wedded to a happy ending as romance. Books can be finished off in many ways – with a shrug, a rueful smile or a backward glance of nostalgia, for instance. But not with death, depression or shame. Save the downbeat notes for your literary fiction.

> 'I like happy endings because that's the one thing we can do in fiction. Real life doesn't have happy endings – it goes on and you die.'
>
> Kate Atkinson

Your turn

List the last three novels you have read of any type. Try and analyse their structure.

Is the narrative straightforward?

Does it have a beginning, a middle and an end – in that order?

How many narrative strands are there?

Does the storyline flash back in time?

If so, how do you feel about it?

Do you want to skip it and read on? Or does it enrich the experience of reading the book?

Take these three novels (or any others – it doesn't matter) and look closely at the first few pages.

Do they arrest your attention at once or do they build in a leisurely fashion? (If they start slowly, check when they were written – the nineteenth-century novel didn't need to take off like a sprinter to prevent the reader reaching for the TV remote control or the modem connection.)

Is it immediately clear what is going on and what kind of book this is?

You could try this experiment in a book shop on novels you are not familiar with. It's a method used by many to select their holiday reading.

Consider your own novel in the light of these issues:

Have you decided on a location?

How unusual is it?

Are you sure the reason you're setting your novel in a Parisian whorehouse/Moorish harem/the Venice Lido is not because you read a sexy book set there last week?

Have you chosen the world of television as your background because you have some personal insight into it – or because you fancy all the presenters currently on the box?

If you have actually completed your novel, is the ending satisfactory – in every sense?

Are all the plot strands resolved?

Are the reader's expectations fulfilled?

Have you ended on an upbeat note?

5
PEOPLE

> 'The Texan turned out to be good-natured, generous and likeable. In three days no one could stand him.'
>
> Joseph Heller, *Catch-22* (1961)

Who cares?

It is a given in all fiction that the characters – particular the protagonist – must be of interest. If the reader does not care what happens to them then he or she will not bother to turn the page. And that, as they say, is the end of the story – probably two hundred pages too soon.

Your characters can be saintly, sadistic, virtuous, vile, defective or devious – anything, in fact, but boring. And if it is important to your book that your protagonist is a bore, then you have to write it in such a way that the book itself is not boring (George and Weedon Grosssmith's *The Diary of a Nobody*, for example).

It helps, of course, if the reader can personally identify with a character and thus feel their pains and pleasures at first hand. In many famous instances, the author's own identification with the central character is plain, which does not prevent the reader feeling a special empathy too. *Jane Eyre* and *David Copperfield* are well-known examples of books whose protagonists speak to succeeding generations of admirers almost on an individual basis.

What of erotica then? Is it necessary to empathise with the characters? Considering that people in an erotic novel are required to make love on cue (once a chapter, at least), can we expect them to be any more than robots programmed to fornicate indiscriminately? Is the erotic novelist simply required to create decorative ciphers?

The answer to this is, of course, no. In erotica, the same general principles of character creation apply – within the restrictions of the genre. So, though the hunky hero with the ever-ready eight-inch erection has a certain crude appeal to the male reader, that reader will expect a bit more in the personality department. If it is obvious that the guy will get the girl and bring her to multiple orgasm every time then events will be predictable – and predictable equals boring. Similarly, if your heroine is a raving nymphomaniac on page one, willing to bed anyone over the age of consent, the reader is likely to be left cold no matter how intense the sex scenes that follow.

In erotica, it is understood that the characters have a capacity to make a lot of love. It's not whether they're going to do it but why and how they yield that makes the act exciting. Though you don't have to be Dostoevsky to create an effective erotic hero or heroine, these days it is not enough for your protagonist simply to be an animated sex organ. The more intriguing your characters, the greater the reader's involvement – in erotica as in any other kind of fiction.

Dead or alive

I'm sure you'll have concluded from your own reading that erotic scenes acquire much more power if the participants are not simply beautiful bodies, however inventively entwined. The standard advice to novelists in general is: know your characters. You should be aware of how and where they grew up, their interests and ambitions, whether they take sugar in their coffee and what radio station they tune in to in the car. Naturally these minutiae are for your eyes only – it's the Iceberg Theory at work once more.

This advice is also applicable to the erotic writer though I'd caution against getting carried away. For practical purposes – time being money – there's no point in creating detailed biographies of the entire cast. Knowing what the heroine's best friend read at university is not relevant when her function in the plot is to pose as a stripper at the hero's stag night to test his fidelity (unless, of course, this knowledge is the key to her character, as far as you are concerned).

The kind of thing that *is* relevant to you is how your creations react in their intimate moments. Is she shy or is she bold? Is he modest or vain? Selfish or considerate? A dominant or a submissive? These are the topics an erotic novelist must ponder in relation to his or her characters.

By the time you start writing you will know your heroine's domestic circumstances, how she pays the bills and what she's like in bed. Of these things the most important is the last because that's what your readers want to know – and you must show them in detail. If you fudge it, whatever the other merits of your book, it will fail as an erotic novel.

Erotic character development

Novelists and critics set great store by character development. The traditionally successful novel is a journey of experience for the hero who completes the arc of his travels altered by the passage of events, emerging wiser or humbler, happier or sadder, enriched or diminished by self-knowledge – at any rate, *changed*. And the reader shares this journey with the protagonist and is enriched by proxy. Thus Dorothea in *Middlemarch*, Paul in *All Quiet on the Western Front*, Winston Smith in *1984* and so on.

Character development on this scale is necessarily curtailed in erotica. Yet it can't be denied that characters are changed by their multifarious experiences in sex books – O, for example, in *The Story of O* and any number of other once-innocents who emerge from these stories in touch with their true sexual natures.

Inevitably, character development in this genre is measured in terms of erotic progression. Whatever your characters' level of sexual experience at the outset of the novel it must be enlarged by the events of the narrative. The action requires that the protagonist swims in deeper waters than he or she has previously ventured into. This notion of doing things you haven't done before is a basic appeal of the genre and caters directly to the reader as voyeur.

Similarly, the nature of a character's sexuality may change in the course of the action as, through new sensual experience, he or she acquires more self-knowledge. In Cathryn Cooper's *Temptation*, for example, though the heroine is a sexual adventuress she can only reach orgasm in the arms of a lover by fantasising about Rudolph Valentino. Then she meets Etienne and suddenly she has no need of Valentino – a turn of events that tells her, and us, that this is the man she really cares for.

Non-sexual motivation

In erotic novels men and women don't just perform sex acts because they desire the other party. As we have discussed, sex is the currency of these books and through sexual behaviour the players act out the drama of the story. There are many reasons why men and women have sexual relations beyond mutual attraction: ambition, revenge, blackmail, espionage and so on. Similarly there are many emotions to be experienced as well as desire: jealousy, anger, sorrow – you can extend the list, I'm sure.

Furthermore, character and plot cannot be discussed in isolation. The situations in which you place your characters and how they react to them will signify what sort of people they are. It is what people do that makes them interesting and brings them to life.

Here's an expanded example. In Carl Mariner's *The Sex Files: Beyond Limits* (1997), para-sexual investigator Bonny Jarvis meets an informer in a strip club. So far we have been told that Jarvis regards sexual activity with scientific detachment. Lovelace, her informer, is anathema to her and to meet him in such a sleazy environment is particularly loathsome. Yet she goes because he has information she wants.

> He grasped her hand and pulled it towards him. His hand was huge and hairy, like a bear's paw, and his grip was like iron. She was powerless to resist as he thrust it beneath the table. It met bare flesh. His fly was open and his erect penis speared upwards from his belly.
>
> The organ was vast: a rock-hard column of flesh, hot to the touch. He pressed her hand against it.

'I won't,' she said.

'Then why did you come? You know the rules, Bonny.'

And so she did. She took a deep breath and curled her fingers around the shaft of his cock, it was so broad she could hardly circle it. He released his grip on her hand.

'That's better. I believe you've got magic fingers.'

'You know I hate you, don't you, Lovelace?'

'Sure. That's what makes this fun. Do you think you could stroke me just a little harder?'

'You disgust me.'

'I know. Ooh, that's nice. Perhaps I'll call you Jerk-Off Jarvis. You do it better than anyone I know.'

If Jarvis had enjoyed masturbating Lovelace – which is what you might expect in an overtly erotic book – then this scene would be much less interesting (and less titillating too). The fact that she loathes him but she does it anyway reveals a lot about her: that she is sexually discriminating, that she is tough and that she will do *anything* to crack a case. The irony is that Jarvis is damned good at giving sexual pleasure – 'you've got magic fingers' – and the reader knows she will have to come to terms with her suppressed sensual impulses before the end of the book.

Recognising your characters' needs

'When human beings love they try to get something.'

E. M. Forster, *Aspects of the Novel* (1927)

In life everyone has an individual set of priorities, so too in fiction. It helps sometimes for a writer to list them. In erotica, it's useful to see what your characters' motivations are so you can exploit them to the full. Ask yourself what each character in your novel wants and write it down – like this analysis of the cast of *Lust on the Line* (1996) by Noel Amos, a novel set in the (entirely fantasy) world of erotic publishing.

LUCIAN (an editor): wants to keep his job and steer clear of women

MIRANDA (Lucian's new boss): wants to turn the loss-making Whimsical Press into a success by publishing sex books

CAROLINE (Lucian's former lover): wants Lucian to publish her novel – and to satisfy her masochistic fantasies

TANIA (an author): wants hands-on input from her editor (Lucian)

KAREN (a trophy wife): wants to get revenge on her philandering, literary-novelist husband (Monty) by publishing an embarrassing erotic confession

MARILYN (Karen's agent): wants to sell Karen's book for pots of money – and turn Lucian into her sex slave in the process

MONTY: wants to keep his trophy wife (Karen) and mistress (Harriet) *and* win a coveted literary award, the Baxendale Prize

HARRIET: wants to bribe all the Baxendale judges with her lush body so she can win Monty the prize and take Karen's place

What is clear from this, if you are familiar with the novel, is the extent to which the characters fail to achieve their goals. Lucian, for example, is recovering from an unhappy love affair and wants no truck with sex or demanding women. But Miranda demands he assemble an erotic publishing programme and suddenly his life is filled with obscene texts and sexy authors with an agenda of their own – as the list above reveals. Naturally events conspire and Lucian is thrust into carnal situations from which he is not strong enough to extricate himself.

From an author's point of view, it is illuminating to record the main characters' motivations in this way. Keep the list as simple as possible. If you can't express a person's *raison d'être* in one sentence – or if you can't give them a motivation at all – it may indicate a weakness or that you haven't thought matters through to their conclusion. In erotica, of course, it's quite sufficient to ascribe a secondary character's driving force as simply 'wants to get laid'.

Licence to indulge

In the real world, we do not usually yield to temptation without paying a price. Invariably this means damage to the waistline, bank account or personal relationships. In fiction, however, we can vicariously indulge our vices and in erotic fiction we do so through characters like the editor, Lucian, who is simply too weak to say no. As erotic author Tom Crewe says, 'The people in my books are awful – but I can't help liking them.'

Flawed personalities are, of course, the stuff of any fiction but it is important that their transgressions are understandable. 'Come off it,' you may think. 'It doesn't matter who has who in these books, the act is all that counts.'

Well, you're right – up to a point. There are many published erotic novels that pay not the slightest lip-service to the conventions of acceptable behaviour. Everyone jumps everyone else's bones without a murmur of protest. I find this less effective than if the people concerned know they are behaving badly and go ahead and do it anyway. It seems to me that this is more plausible and the characters consequently more sympathetic. One of the skills in writing in a genre where the cast are required to behave in an outlandish way is to make that behaviour credible. And any steps the novelist can take to aid the suspension of disbelief will result in a more satisfied reader.

For example, if the heroine, on her wedding day, cheerfully allows herself to be screwed by a previous boyfriend, no matter the quality of the orgasm she will risk alienating the reader. If, on the other hand, in response to a heartfelt appeal, she succumbs despite herself, in anguish and guilt as well as excitement, bestowing one last carnal gift on a spurned lover, then we understand her weakness and feel for her.

Pauline closed her eyes and groaned in despair. She was being so weak. So terribly, terminally weak. She wasn't doing anything to resist. She knew the problem, of course: the orders emanating from her heavily lubricating pussy were directly contrary to those from her brain. And not for the first time in her life – more like the hundred and first. 'We mustn't do it, Mark!' she stammered, feeling a puff of breeze from the window wafting coolly across her near-naked, up-turned rear end.

The Perils of Pauline Peach, Alison North (1988)

Essential characters

Every genre has its cast of familiar characters. Spy thrillers are inhabited by cynical loners and urbane puppet-masters; clogs-and-shawl sagas contain impoverished heroines and devious mill-owners; detective mysteries have slow-witted policemen and brilliant amateur sleuths.

Erotica is no different in this respect. It has its own particular stereo-types. And though your first reaction will probably be a desire to avoid them at all costs there is little point in striving for complete originality. Stereotypes exist for a reason in every style of fiction. The dynamics of erotica require a balance of innocence and depravity that is reflected in the *dramatis personae* of the novels themselves.

If you analyse erotic novels you have read, or maybe the one you are working on now, you will find they contain some of the following people:

Group 1
The innocent on a journey to sexual awareness
The modest woman whose sensual nature has been neglected
The amateur whore

Group 2
The wealthy *roué*
The sophisticated sadist

The female dominant
The amoral young man
The rich bitch who likes a bit of rough

Group 3
The bit of rough
The daring best friend who eggs the protagonist on
The benevolent mentor
The vocational whore

The protagonist is likely to come from the first group (in Becky Bell's *Amateur Nights*, mentioned earlier, she is all three); and the villain, or opposing character, from the second. The third group comprises secondary characters, though they are often significant. The benevolent mentor, for example, can be an older woman who initiates the hero into the mysteries of sex. The best friend is often a significant companion on the heroine's journey, being both a dramatic foil and a sexual catalyst. It is usual for the friend's virtue to weigh less than the protagonist's and you should note, if they are female, that they are likely to end up in bed together.

It is worth noting that the convention in heterosexual erotica is that women may swap sexual preferences but that men must stick to the opposite sex. The explanation for this double standard is that, though the notion of female bisexuality is titillating for the male reader, similar behaviour in men is liable to turn that same reader off. Given the relatively high proportion of female readers of male lists (based on the Delta statistics) and the number of female authors at work this may not be so strictly observed in the future. But, for the moment, the rule in 'male' erotica is that though Rosalind may bunk up with Celia – and readers would be disappointed if she didn't – Hamlet must keep his hands off Horatio. When they said all was fair in love and war they weren't referring to straight male erotica.

Viewpoint

'In my books, I try and get in people's heads and feel what they are feeling.'

Carol Anderson

Erotica is by definition an intimate genre. It requires the constant description of sexual acts whose significance can only really be appreciated by those engaged in them. To be effective, the writer should be able to put the reader inside the skins of his passionately embracing characters. Unless the reader can share some of that passion, he or she will not be involved in the book.

First person

> He now lost what little self-restraint was left to him. He
> caught me in his strong arms. He rubbed his body against
> mine. He kissed me on the mouth. Our tongues met – my
> eyes looked into his. He read desire – hot, voluptuous desire,
> there. We both groaned to indulge it – to enjoy – to satisfy
> it. We were mad, but there was method in our madness.
>
> *Eveline*, Anonymous (c.1840)

Eveline, like much pornography from previous eras, is written in the first person. It's an effective means of giving the reader the protagonist's first-hand experience. Of course, when writing an 'I narrative', that's all you can give without resorting to a variety of awkward devices ('she told me later what had gone on at Grace's party when...' etc.). What your character sees and feels in person is all that can be directly conveyed. In erotica, this means your hero or heroine must participate in, or watch, every sexual encounter.

There's one other factor you might like to consider. If you write in the first person, your character's adventures will inevitably appear to be your own. Even if you use a pseudonym – I'll come to that issue later – anyone who knows you and reads it may well make the assumption that at least some of the action is autobiographical.

Third person

> Little thrills were rippling through Adrian's belly and
> with a sigh of unalloyed delight he put his hand between
> her thighs, where the skin was like satin, and felt up into

> her loose silk knickers. The moment was here – that soul-shaking moment before he touched her most secret place.
>
> *Love Italian Style*, Anonymous (1991)

Adrian's story is relayed in the third person, a technique that places more distance between the reader and the principal character. In this instance, the novel is told exclusively from Adrian's point of view, which imposes the same constraints as a first-person narrative, in other words, Adrian is in every scene.

The advantage of the third person is that it allows the author to switch viewpoints. Generally speaking, if you wish to tell your tale from one point of view and you feel comfortable with that character's 'voice' then you will opt for the first person. But if you want to get inside more than one person's head then you will choose the third person. Like this:

> Mila fought the feelings of rising pleasure, but they were too powerful. It was much too late to close her mind to the flood of sensations, the burning swell that filled her belly, stiffened her nipples and turned her clitoris into a throbbing seed of ecstasy.
>
> Hobart watched with breathless excitement. Outwardly he was in control, the absolute master, but inside he burned in a hell of jealous desire, yearning to take Mila back from Ronstein and have her all to himself.
>
> *The Golden Cage*, Aurelia Clifford (1995)

This story-telling method requires more discipline. Shifting the point of view within a scene, as here, can confuse the reader if not skilfully contrived. And if the point of view moves back and forth between two or more characters you are likely to lose the entire focus of events and the reader's attention into the bargain. Unless you are very confident of your effects, I'd advise that you stick to one viewpoint. If you wish to convey a different character's impression, put a line space in your text and write the sequence from inside that person's head.

It is necessary to be aware, at any point in your story, through whose eyes you are seeing events. The author should always know whose scene this is, whose chapter this is, whose book this is. This sounds more daunting in theory than it is in practice. But even though the third-person, multiple-viewpoint technique may require more thinking, it is an effective method of telling a story. The scope it gives the author for looking into the minds of his characters is enormous. It is also unique to the novel. Film and TV are wonderful narrative media with many advantages – every picture tells a story, after all – but they can't reveal a character's thought processes like a novel.

You may feel inhibited about assuming the point of view of someone of the opposite sex. Give it a try. If you find you can't do it with conviction, then don't. Some lists specify the viewpoint they wish their writers to adopt. On the whole, women's erotica (see Chapter 8) requires novels to be written from a predominately female point of view, while male lists are happy with either. The assumption is that men can be turned on by looking at sexual behaviour through a woman's eyes while women are less likely to enjoy a masculine perspective – which may or may not be true.

This raises the interesting question of how much the gender of the writer has a bearing on the successful realisation of characters of the opposite sex.

There are women's lists that won't take work from men, which is, I assume, more of a marketing ploy than an honest belief that male writers cannot invent female characters. Fanny Hill, after all, was created by a man; so, too, Becky Sharp, Anna Karenina and Madame Bovary (as sexy a collection of heroines as you could hope to meet outside the erotic genre). Of course, female authors have also created powerfully attractive males – Mr Darcy, Heathcliff, Rhett Butler. What it comes down to is that gender alone will not prohibit you from realising convincing characters of the opposite sex. Skill, imagination and accurate observation of human nature are, of course, another matter.

A final word on viewpoint. Though the third person, in particular, means the author can play God, these days God does not have a speaking part. It is unlikely you will be tempted to address your readers directly, like a grand Victorian novelist. And, though advice is often profitably ignored, I'd counsel strongly against playing the omnipotent narrator in the manner of George Eliot or Thackeray or, more to the point, the unknown nineteenth-century author of the following:

> We shall not detain our reader long in the lady's bedroom, as the lovers, being calmer than usual after the day's enjoyments, were disposed to be rational, somewhat in the manner of married couples after the honeymoon; so that the proceedings comprised a judicious amount of straightforward fucking, variegated by alternations of refreshing slumber, enjoyed in each other's arms.
>
> *Rosa Fielding*, Anonymous (1856)

No one writes like that these days except when engaged in pastiche or unless they wish to make a point of the technique – see *The French Lieutenant's Woman* by John Fowles. The brilliant narrative dexterity Fowles employs would be wasted in genre writing. Apart from anything else, the self-conscious voice of the omnipotent narrator places yet another barrier between the reader and the characters in the story. In erotica, the more immediate you can make the experience, the more effective your novel will be.

Looks

Given that the nature of this genre requires constant sexual activity, it is imperative that your characters actually are sexy. If you can persuade the reader to desire the people in your drama then you can, at the appropriate moment, satisfy those desires in the action of the book.

One obvious and relatively easy means of achieving this is to make your characters physically attractive. Quite how you do this is down to your skill as a writer and we will discuss descriptive techniques later. However, bear in mind that as a general rule there are no warts in erotica – no running sores, harelips and gross obesity. If this sanitised view of reality offends you, turn to another genre. The biggest sin is to turn the reader off. In the fantasy world of sex books, we are all Michelle Pfeiffer and Daniel Day-Lewis.

Actually, we are more than that. We are also Marilyn Monroe, Diana Ross, Ingrid Bergman, Julia Roberts, Whitney Houston, Clark Gable, Yul Brynner, Mick Jagger, Clint Eastwood, Eddie Murphy, Brad Pitt... The point being, not for you to stuff your book full of celebrated lookalikes but to offer a range of physically diverse types. Remember the third Blue Rule.

In this respect it is useful for the erotic novelist to keep a check-list of physical characteristics. Given that your characters will undoubtedly spend time baring their flesh and generally examining each other's intimate nooks and crannies, you must keep tabs on what they look like. In real life, a lover's body has a special allure. That mole like a chocolate button on her collarbone, the dimples in his tight white buttocks, the heart-shaped swell of her bottom when she's bending to retrieve her stockings... these details are significant and you must not muddle them up.

Write down the name of your character and note the salient physical characteristics: eye colour, hair colour, breast shape, cock size – whatever's relevant. A note of where to find previous descriptions in your working manuscript is also useful. Consistency of physical description is important. If your hero's smooth and hairless chest becomes matted with black curly hair in the climactic encounter then your reader will know that you care less about your characters than she does.

Don't expect the publisher's copy-editor to spot this kind of error. He or she may well do but the primary responsibility is yours. The simple thing is to keep the check-list. Start it when you begin the book and add to it as you go along. Though entries such as 'Henrik – barrel chest, blue eyes, cock curved like a banana' may look daft, they could save you a frustrating ten minutes of searching through your work-in-progress when you'd rather be describing how Henrik puts his banana to good use.

Names

For some people, christening their characters is easy. If that's you, skip what follows. Others have a lot of trouble with names or else they do not realise the significance of finding the right one. Certain writers discover that choosing the correct name is the first step in the process of invention and without it they cannot proceed. For these people, the right name *is* the character. Choosing a name can be a surprising stumbling-block in the creation of your novel.

Naming your characters is also a way in which an author can sound a note of originality, a chance to add an extra dimension simply by word association. Yet, as in most things, there are pitfalls peculiar to this genre. Suppose, while checking the proofs of your soon-to-be-published erotic novel, you discover that the whip-wielding, impossibly busted whore-mistress who keeps the heroine in a dungeon for three chapters has the same Christian name as your mother-in-law? How are you going to explain that to your wife who has supported you nobly throughout the writing process? And what are going to say to your best mate, Pete (who has already ordered six copies as spoof Christmas presents), when the guy in your novel with an abnormally small organ of generation is called – oh dear – Pete?

It's imperative that you run a mental check-list over your cast to eliminate any *faux pas* of this sort. The potential for embarrassment is enormous. In particular, don't put in someone's name for a joke – they may not appreciate it; or include it out of malice – the consequences could be dangerous. (A discussion of libel and other legal topics follows in Chapter 9.)

There is a corollary to this: some people are overjoyed to see their names in print, even – maybe especially – in this context. If you intend to flatter anyone in this way make sure you talk to them about it first. One author I know claims his friends love being recognised in his novels. Nevertheless, I would not advise including anyone of your acquaintance in your book, either wittingly or not.

Christening your characters

'Choosing a name is one of the novelist's bugbears. A character will not answer to the wrong name.'

L. P. Hartley

There are four common ways of thinking up names:

1. The thin-air method

You pop down the first name that flashes into your head. Often this is just the label you need though it's worth trying to examine where the inspiration came from. This is where most unwitting errors of the kind noted above can occur. When you finally realise that Dominique appeals to you because of a pen-friend you corresponded with at school you can proceed happily. On the other hand, if this is the name of next door's au pair maybe you should rethink.

2. The Dickensian method

The author invents a name that encapsulates some of the personality of the character, for example Mrs Gamp, Mr Pecksniff, Inspector Bucket. This is an entertaining and sometimes effective means of enlivening your novel though care should be taken when adapting this method to erotica. Dickens was not literal in its use. His characters' unique names add something without being obvious. It would be too crude to call your heroine Patsy Pertbum. Patsy Pert, on the other hand, could be just what you are looking for. This form of appellation is most suitable to historical or satirical novels. It should be used subtly.

3. The anonymous method

The idea is to render the characters' names unimportant in comparison to their deeds. Their labels are so common – Sam, Bill, Dick, Sue, Jane, Anne etc. – that they could be anyone. No one could take offence at their name being used in this way. There are millions of Mikes in the world so why should I think you mean me?

4. The exotic method

Some authors swear by the unusual: Delphine, Alessandro, Kasim, Carezza, Ineni, Casilda and so on. In the right context, imports from another culture can be telling, adding a touch of the exotic to the atmosphere. If you are stuck for a seductive name, you could do worse than simply think French – Anaïs, Eugénie, Raoul, André, Camille...

Though the charm of a name, like beauty and obscenity, is in the eye of the beholder, it is important to try to select names for your characters that are not a handicap. Prosaic labels like Mavis Tubbs, Doreen Smith, Ron Pratt – or Mike Bailey, for that matter – are not dramatic or seductive or sweet-sounding to any degree. Your characters' names can be soft or hard, powerful or decorative but, in this genre, it's no surprise to learn that they must be sexy. Junk Doris, Cora, Oswald and Don, think Sylvie, Tamsin, Luc and Stéfan.

A name plays a further function in the mind of the reader. Failing all else, it differentiates one character from another. You must make sure your characters' names are different. This may seem a laughable piece of advice but some erotic novels use up bodies like First World War generals. It is easy to forget that the voluptuous waitress who served herself as dessert on page ten bears the same name as the society hostess with the irresistible fund-raising technique a hundred pages later. Some readers will be aware of this and charge you with laziness – for which you have no defence.

You should also ensure that there's enough variety – the third Blue Rule – in the names you use. Sometimes they can be so similar as to spread confusion. I have read a novel submitted for publication in which the principal female characters were called Penny, Poppy and Philippa – or Pip, for short. As a result, it was not easy to tell exactly whose wellspring of sensuality was being plumbed at any given time.

In the same way that you should avoid giving all your male characters dark hair and soulful brown eyes, you should keep track of how their names sound. When the heroine falls for Hugo after a tryst with Nico, soon to be followed by dinner with Ivo then the reader will feel short-changed. Even if there *is* only one kind of name that sets your literary juices flowing, you should disguise the fact and sometimes call your man Sebastian (or whatever).

Most of your quandaries to do with names can be solved by one simple purchase – a book of first names of the kind acquired by expectant parents. If you can find one that lists by category, so much the better (you can turn straight to the Russian section to name your ballet-loving heroine) though any decent listing will do. A thesaurus (for the Dickensian method), telephone directories and historical biographies (for the period novelist) are also useful but I wouldn't swap any of them for my copy of *Beyond Jennifer and Jason* by Rosencrantz and Satran (St Martin's Press, 1988).

Your turn

1. Look at this passage:

> The chattering faded for a second when he entered the party. Brett knew he had been noticed – his physical presence always had that effect on a room full of women. A girl was already in front of him, pushing her soft breasts into his chest, saying how great it was to see him again. He did not acknowledge her. Instead his gaze swept the room like a search-light. He caught the eye of a redhead in a silk dress. She seemed to float through the crowd towards him.

> 'Hi,' she said. 'I'm Bethany.'

> Brett nodded. He put his hand on her waist and felt the heat of her skin through the thin material. 'Tonight's your lucky night, sweetheart,' he said. 'I'm going to fuck your brains out.'

Now address these questions:

Did you like Brett?

Did you find him interesting?

Would you want to read a novel with him as the central character?

If not, why not?

How could you alter the text to make him more sympathetic?

2. Think of a reason for two people to be in bed together in addition to the sexual attraction they feel for each other. Create a scenario around this and invent the characters. Name them. What do they want, apart from sex? Describe them. If sufficiently inspired, go ahead and write the scene from one point of view, in the first person. Rewrite it in the third person, conveying the feelings of both parties.

3. Alternatively, analyse the novel you are working on in the light of the issues raised in this chapter.

4. Ask these questions about the names of characters in your novel:

   (a) Are you sure you have not used a name that will cause embarrassment to anyone of your acquaintance who may read your work?

   (b) Are the names of your characters sufficiently dissimilar to avoid confusion?

   (c) Are the names you have chosen sexy enough?

   If you answer 'no' to any of these, do something about it right away.

6

THE NITTY-GRITTY

> 'Is erotic fiction dirty? Only if it's done right.'
>
> After Woody Allen
> *Everything You Always Wanted To Know About Sex* (1972)

Style

Though not all would agree with me, I believe there are as many ways of writing an erotic novel as there are of writing any kind of fiction. Maybe I'm idealistic but I like to think that sexually arousing events can be successfully conveyed in most writing styles and that the freedom of expression that is available to writers as a result is one of the attractions of the erotic genre. In other words, the author has options and there is no formulaic way of achieving results (although you may get a different impression from some of the end product on sale).

That said, when Delta canvassed opinions on style, the results were as follows:

Preferred writing style	
Hardcore	35%
Realistic	24%
No preference	19%
Humorous	10%
Romantic	6%
Hard-boiled	4%
Ironic	2%

The categories may require a word of explanation.

Hardcore

Hardcore is a powerful term that conjures up images of visceral no-frills sex. When the police seize obscene magazines or videos they are invariably described as 'hardcore'. Hold the foreplay, ditch the euphemisms, gimme cock-and-cunt action all the way – that's the promise. In practice, there's as much tease in this vein as any other and Henry Miller, the father of this style, was a pyrotechnical phrase-maker of brilliance.

> In a jiffy she had opened the door and was groping about in the dark to find the couch. I didn't say a word, I didn't make a move. I just kept my mind riveted on her cunt moving quietly in the dark like a crab. Finally she was standing beside the couch. She didn't say a word either. She just stood there quietly and as I moved my hand up her legs she moved one foot a little to open her crotch a bit more. I don't think I ever put my hand into such a juicy crotch in all my life. It was like paste running down her legs, and if there had been any billboards handy I could have plastered up a dozen or more. After a few moments, just as naturally as a cow lowering its head to graze, she bent over and put it in her mouth. I had my whole four fingers inside her, whipping it up to a froth. Her mouth was stuffed full and the juice pouring down her legs. Not a word out of us, as I say. Just a couple of quiet maniacs working away in the dark like gravediggers. It was a fucking Paradise and I knew it...
>
> *Tropic of Capricorn*, Henry Miller (1939)

Realistic

In stylistic terms this is similar to 'hardcore' with an emphasis on credibility. As one respondent to the survey said, 'I like to feel that somewhere, some time it happened.'

I turned round to start the music over and when I turned back Steph was kissing Ivan. It was like a punch in the gut. She had a hand in his hair, pulling his face into hers. Their mouths were working, probing and tasting each other. I was stunned. I watched the hem of her shirt ride up to bare the pale flesh of her midriff. My heart was pounding like a hammer.

My mind was racing too. Suddenly it seemed obvious that I was an intruder. Maybe they had planned an afternoon in bed together and I'd turned up out of the blue. I stood up shakily and slipped out of the door. I felt noble as I did so. Noble and frustrated.

Faithless Lady, from *Eroticon Heat*, ed J.-P. Spencer (1997)

Humorous

There's a school of thought that decrees that humour has no place in erotica. For my part, I like a laugh, both in bed and in bedroom literature, though it is a difficult trick to tickle the erogenous zone and the funny bone at the same time. Of course, quite a few giggles can be gained from work that is not intentionally funny. The key thing to bear in mind if you actively seek to be humorous is not to signal your purpose. No character in a Tom Sharpe novel believes that life is one big joke, they are all deadly serious about the farcical situations they find themselves in. The moment that a character signals to the reader, 'This is a bit of a laugh', the soufflé collapses. Traditionally, 'humour' in erotica denotes a jolly men's-club tone, as in the excerpt that follows. Maybe you can do better in a modern vein – ten per cent of readers specifically enjoy it, after all.

An awakening in a whore's bedroom is, as a rule, cheerless. One is vague as to one's whereabouts, as a rule sore on the John Thomas and a general feeling of having made a bloody fool of one's self is most often mixed with a

> wonder whose pyjamas you've got on, and whether you've got the clap – or possibly worse.
>
> *Maudie*, Anonymous (1909)

Romantic

This is a much-abused term, often the source of cheap jibes from those who can think no further than the confections of Barbara Cartland (whose commercial success few can afford to sneer at). But romantic writing covers a great deal of ground, a lot of which seems to me ideally suited to erotica. Heightened emotions and sensual awareness, a flight from life's realities, faith in the heart over the head – all these elements lend themselves to effective and passionate sexy writing.

> Sobbing with pleasure, she felt him begin the hypnotic electric dance of his orgasm. As he pressed deeper the pleasures were mirrored within her. Suddenly, almost before she had time to think, she was there with him, riding out into the darkness, feeling her body contracting rhythmically around him. Every thought, every sensation was centred on the junction of their two bodies. She gave herself totally and let the heat drown out all thoughts except the pleasure and the power of the desire between them.
>
> *A Private Affair*, Carol Anderson (1995)

Hardboiled

The style of American pulp fiction, raised to an art form in the work of writers like Raymond Chandler, can also be borrowed by the erotic novelist. The difficulty is that the wise-guy tone and the unrelenting search for the snappy simile can sometimes intrude to the detriment of the reader's involvement. However, the style carries with it cultural baggage (those Bogart movies) that can, in the right circumstances, work to the writer's advantage. And the right circumstances invariably mean a private eye and an unhappy woman:

Mrs Mountjoy – Marilyn by now because we'd had lots of tearful should-I-shouldn't-I? conversations and I was up there in her pantheon of father confessors along with her shrink and her gynaecologist – Marilyn had said her husband, Clyde, was a sucker for European women with big breasts. So, despite my worries about using Bella as bait – her lack of experience in the world of subterfuge and surveillance etc – I decided to give her a crack at Clyde. After all, I thought, she may not know a damn thing about the divorce laws or how to bug a phone but I'd bet a doughnut to a diamond pinkie ring that she'd had a lot of experience at cosying up to guys in bars.

'Crazy Time', from *Eroticon Fever*, ed J.-P. Spencer (1995)

Ironic

The novelist most associated with irony is Jane Austen but the subtle variations of tone that reveal to the reader the discrepancy between appearance and reality are employed by almost all writers at some point. Though the erotic novelist's chief concern is to thrill his readers that doesn't mean he cannot amuse them from time to time by making distinctions about their behaviour. In the right context, irony and its associated techniques of exaggeration, sarcasm and satire can be usefully employed – not necessarily to make a moral judgement but possibly just to raise a smile. Erotic readers, as I hope has been established, are no less perceptive than anyone else.

For a woman of her maturity, Joyce's bosom was indeed magnificent, with just a little sag and spread which, to many an appreciative eye, only added to its character. And Danny's eye was indeed appreciative. He grasped a big tit in each hand and pressed his face into the beckoning valley between, muttering as he did so, 'England!' Joyce tenderly stroked the back of his head; she was easily moved by a show of patriotic sentiment.

Lust on the Loose, Noel Amos (1993)

Because Delta is a 'male' list there is another influential voice not represented here – woman's 'language of the senses'. Anaïs Nin wrote dollar-a-page pornography in the early 1940s for an unknown collector. Though the collector was a man who sent messages urging her to 'be specific' and to 'leave out the poetry', the results represent sexual experience from a woman's point-of-view.

He parted her legs as if he wanted to break them apart. His hair fell on her face. Smelling it, she felt the orgasm coming and called out to him to increase his thrusts so that they could come together. At the moment of the orgasm he cried out in a tiger's roar, a tremendous sound of joy, ecstasy and furious enjoyment such as she had never heard. It was as she had imagined the Arab would cry, like some jungle animal, satisfied with his prey, who roars with pleasure. She opened her eyes. Her face was covered with his black hair. She took it into her mouth.

Delta of Venus, Anaïs Nin (1940/1, published 1969)

From the variety of the quoted material above I hope you can see that the mansion of erotica has many rooms. And if you are skilful there is a corner here for you too. Within reason, erotica will allow you to find your own voice and that should be your ambition.

The language of sex

It would be a mistake to take the survey results I have quoted too literally. If you did that then you might be misled into thinking I am advising you to write in the vein of Henry Miller. That's not my intention. The definitions are simply my explanation of those category terms – quite how the respondents interpreted such shorthand is another matter. The preference, such as it is, for 'hardcore' to me reflects the strength of the word. It also sums up a basic desire for sexual excitement. These readers do not want a novel that is coy about the physical aspects of sex. They want it described in explicit detail.

'How's the book going?' asked Brendan.

Percy pushed his notepad across the table without comment. It would be interesting to see Brendan's reaction. He, after all, was the target audience.

The Irishman eyed the top page and his face fell. He took another gulp of beer and his brow furrowed in concentration.

'What does "callypygian" mean, Percy?'

'Having beautifully shaped buttocks.'

'And "cyprian sceptre"?'

'That's a penis.'

'So what this bit means is the sight of her pretty arse made his cock go stiff?'

'Yes.'

'Then, for God's sake, man, why don't you say so? Do you expect people to read your book with a dictionary in the other hand? How the hell are they going to jerk off?'

Lust on the Line, Noel Amos (1996)

Realms of bliss

Quite what language are you going to use in your novel? You've outlined your plot, conjured up some characters, envisaged the opening sequence – are you now itching to fill the page with the most vivid obscenities you can think of? Or are you going to have a failure of nerve?

You should know that there are erotic novelists who never use the basic sex terms. Supporters of *Fanny Hill* frequently remind us that there is no 'bad language' in the book at all. The anonymous author of the Eros series – *Eros in the Town, Eros in the Country,* etc. – has no recourse to explicit labels; neither has the prolific writer who masquerades under the pseudonyms of Anne-Marie Villefranche, Marie-Claire Villefranche, Margarete von Falkensee and many more (her books include the *Plaisir D'Amour, Amour, Amour* and *Blue Angel Nights* series). It is surprising how graphic an imaginative writer can be using simple euphemisms for sex organs such as part, stamen, stem, staff, spike (for penis) and place, peach, inlet, split, slit (for vagina). It is also possible to invent an individual vocabulary of sex terms tailored to a particular book.

'Feel that!' he said, grinning wolfishly at her.

Odette smiled slyly as she took hold – strength and stiffness had returned and the warm length of flesh twitched in her fingers. Jacques slid his own free hand between her bare thighs to touch her *little heart* and she sighed. With impatient fingers Jacques prised the wet lips of her *joujou* open and pushed a fingertip inside to stroke her. She was slippery and hot to his touch.

Bonjour Amour, Marie-Claire Villefranche (1995)

But for most writers, especially those whose books have a contemporary setting, the basic words we use for body parts and sexual activity are essential. Words such as cock, prick, rod, dick, cunt, pussy, quim, hole and so on. And, though an entire novel that restricted itself to the vocabulary of a doctor's surgery might have something of a cold-blooded quality, anatomical terms are also useful – penis, vagina, testicles, semen, anus etc. Particular note should also be made of that versatile word 'sex' which can be usefully applied to both male and female genitalia.

Turn-on terms

Progressing into the hot zone, there are common phrases that, though clichéd, go to the heart of the mainstream erotic novel. Used at the appropriate moment, phrases such as 'big tits', 'wet cunt', 'thick cock' have a visceral appeal that pushes many a reader's buttons. This is the time-honoured 'male' vocabulary of the changing room, the men's magazine and the lavatory wall – basic, in-your-face and, in the right context, still powerful. If your novel is aimed at the traditionally conceived men's market then you will be using buzz phrases like these in your work.

But just making free with rude words is not going to turn you into a successful writer of erotica. My advice is to use the Anglo-Saxon with some sensitivity but don't spare it when the time is right.

> 'I dislike books which rely on bad language as a *substitute* for real eroticism, bad language is however essential *in the right place and context.*'
>
> Male respondent to sex survey

An erotic novel is made up of key sex moments cunningly woven into a plot. And no matter how skilful your writing, how sympathetic your characters or how clever your plot, the book will live or die on the effectiveness of those moments. They are there to give the reader a thrill and if you don't provide it then that reader will feel let down.

At the climax of each one of these key scenes will be, surprise surprise, another climax – probably a mutual one. Though it may have been preceded by any number of minor excitements, there will usually be one significant eruption that the reader, through the blissed-out senses of the fortunate protagonist, will be invited to share. It is in the build-up to this event, as the tease turns to strip and any vestiges of conventional repression are swept away on a tidal wave of sensuality, that the plain language of sex is most needed.

> Under the dress, she wore nothing but a skimpy black garter belt and the sheer black stockings. Her nipples

were stiff, pointed, aggressive, two dark eyes above the furry patch of dark hair covering her sex.

Her body continued to move, her hips gyrating to the beat of the hard rock music.

'I'm getting hot,' she said. 'Getting hot for you... feeling good... my cunt is wet, Michael... wet and wanting... you're going to fuck me later, aren't you?... fuck it hard... oh God!...'

Hearing the words from her red lips, he trembled and almost came.

Three Women, Jocelyn Joyce (1991)

A small digression – note the woman's dress in this extract. In real life, women only wear stockings on special occasions and they usually bitch about it – we all know they'd rather be wearing tights. In erotica, however, stockings are *de rigueur*.

'Seamed stockings aren't subtle but they certainly do the job. You shouldn't wear them when out with someone you're not prepared to sleep with, since their presence is tantamount to saying, "Hi there, big fellow, please rip my clothes off at the earliest opportunity."'

Cynthia Heimel, *Sex Tips for Girls* (1983)

Turn-off terms

'Literature is mostly about having sex and not much about having children; life is the other way around.'

David Lodge, *The British Museum is Falling Down* (1965)

Erotica is not set in the real world, it creates a fantasy version in which sexual pleasure is the birthright of all. An effective erotic novel is like a feel-good Hollywood romance in which the beautiful girl dumps her fiancé to run off with a stranger she's heard on a late-night phone-in. And when the pair finally meet on the top of the Empire State building, our hearts are lifted at the triumph of romance over reason. We know it's all complete hokum – hearing someone on the radio is no basis for a relationship – but, for the duration of the movie (*Sleepless in Seattle*), we *want* the fantasy to be real. It's the same thing with erotica. Mad moments with strangers in half-lit bedrooms, affairs with well-off and well-hung heros, hot nights with honey-thighed heroines open to any shameless suggestion – it's not the real world but there's a part of us, situated probably between our legs, that would like it to be.

It follows therefore that, just as the cute kid in *Sleepless in Seattle* who brings the lovers together does not have repulsive acne, in erotica there are a number of unmentionables, such as sexually transmitted diseases, post-coital discomfort (apart from well-earned fatigue or weals from sex beatings that are worn as a badge of honour), unwanted pregnancy and realistic emotional fall-out (loss-of-custody of children, depression, suicide). Convention also has it that the books aren't filled with used condoms, sanitary towels and soggy bundles of paper tissues. All sex juices are ambrosial, sex odours are intoxicating and certain words – see below – are taboo.

When you reminisce about your finest sexual moments, I bet you don't dwell on the humdrum elements. You recall the excitement, the bliss, the ecstasy. So it is in erotica. Your characters are above the degrading minutiae. This is life seen through a particular pair of tinted spectacles – blue, I suppose. In this genre, nobody but nobody farts or smells of fish.

So, don't use these words when describing bodies: *slimy*, *pulpy*, *smelly*, *cheesy*, *encrusted* (except regarding jewellery), *doughy*, *slack* – you get the picture, I'm sure. And *never* use 'smegma'.

Safe sex

It's possible to get your literary knickers in a twist over the politics of sex and health. Has everyone in my book got to wear a condom you wonder? It's a reasonable question but the answer is no.

The problem, as we're all aware, is that condoms, no matter how ribbed, coloured and cunningly named, remain obstinately functional. The notion of having to stop the action at crucial moments in your narrative while your hero rolls on his prophylactic is deflating – just like real life in fact (the real life you'd rather forget about while you're reading an erotic book). The truth is that it's bad enough having to deal with condoms in reality without having them intrude into your sex fantasies. I say leave them out. No one ever contracted HIV from reading a book.

> 'The safest sex of all comes not in rubber but in paper covers.'
>
> Martin Amis

To underline the point that erotica is pure fiction, some publishers print a disclaimer on the copyright page of their books. This is worded to the effect that what follows is a sexual fantasy and in the real world readers should practise safe sex. After this health warning for the literal-minded, there usually follows 250 pages of unprotected fornication on an epic scale.

You should be aware that at least one publisher (Black Lace) specifically prohibits the description of body fluids mingling internally. In other words, you can't refer to the heroine's vagina or anus being 'flooded with spunk'. The presumption is that the characters are practising safe sex even though condoms are never mentioned. (Precise instructions as to how this works are included in the Black Lace guidelines, which are available from the publisher.)

The one sub-genre in which condoms and safe sex feature regularly is male gay fiction – though even here reality is often an unwelcome intrusion.

> 'It is my considered opinion that fantasy and imagination need no restraint, that the *thought* of sex without latex is perfectly natural and need not be censored. Pornography exists in this realm of the mind. It is one of the few places where it is utterly safe to entertain any concept of any kind of sexual congress.'
>
> Max Exander

Your turn

Take an erotic situation that interests you. How many ways can you express it? Try two or three of the basic styles described in this chapter. Or examine the style of a writer you admire and try to use that. In all probability you will come up with a hybrid version that is your own way of doing it – which is fine. As mentioned, your aim is to discover your own means of expression rather than an ability to pastiche other writers' voices.

Turn to a passage of sexy writing that works for you. Try and analyse the language the writer is using.

How explicit is it?

Does it become more explicit as matters reach their conclusion?

Are there key words or phrases that have particular erotic power?

7

ESSENTIAL TIPS

'Good writers are those who keep the language efficient. That is to say, keep it accurate, keep it clear.'

Ezra Pound

Your voice

Your style is your unique voice. You will find ways of doing things that suit you and effects you like that can only be achieved by unorthodox methods. So feel free to take any of the advice that follows with a pinch of salt – just examine the reasons why you need further seasoning.

Ninety-nine per cent of the writing skills you need to write erotica you need for any kind of fiction. There are many excellent books available on how to express yourself on paper and they are all relevant to you. I will, however, try and re-focus some basic techniques for the purposes of the erotic writer.

Be specific

This is standard advice to writers: avoid descriptions such as 'he was an attractive man', 'she had a lovely face', 'they had a nice time in bed'. Used in this way, adjectives like 'attractive', 'lovely' and 'nice' are so vague as to be almost meaningless. Try and sketch a precise picture: 'he was tall and rangy with a lock of blue-black hair that he kept flicking out of his piercing blue eyes', 'she had a chipped front tooth and big brown Bambi eyes', 'they did everything in bed that two horny teenagers could think of – except sleep'.

As you can see, I've expanded these descriptions considerably which is necessary if you are to individualise at all. However, it's possible to go overboard in this direction. A page-length description of a character would probably lose a reader's attention – do you really expect anyone to remember this kind of detail?

> She had a crop of freckles across the bridge of her nose and high cheekbones. In moments of stress she would bite the underlip of her wide, curving mouth. Her small hands were unadorned by varnish or jewellery, their nails neatly trimmed with the cuticles exposed in milky half-moons. She wore a navy Patrick Gerard jacket over an oyster silk blouse whose top button was unfastened to reveal a pendant in white gold...

There are two points here. The first is that a description of your characters, particularly your significant characters, is important. Erotica is about the physical impact of flesh on flesh and the sight, smell and texture of your imagined lovers must be conveyed in detail. The reader has carnal expectations of every character you introduce, for obvious reasons. You can't fail those expectations simply by saying he or she is lovely, stunning, gorgeous and so on. It's not enough. So be specific and not only about people. Locations, clothes, scenery – all the 'furniture' of your book counts and adds to the atmosphere for the reader.

The second point is to allow your readers to contribute. A few key details about a character will create a picture that readers can not only carry with them throughout the narrative but which they can personalise. A novelist can't nail down a character like a film-maker. If you refer to your heroine as a redhead then she could resemble anyone from Ann-Margret to Sissy Spacek to Geri Halliwell of the Spice Girls. But a film-maker can only cast one actress and if Gillian Anderson lands the part then that is exactly who the viewer sees. No matter how hard the novelist tries he or she can't exert this degree of control – he can't make the reader see Gillian Anderson. So don't try. By all means supply lots of thrilling physical detail but don't expect it to be interpreted exactly the way you envisage it.

The example I gave above of a too-specific description fails not only because it is too detailed but because it is tedious. It's best not to describe a character like an entry in a catalogue, that is, in a list of statements. One way to avoid this is to look at the newcomer through another's eyes.

> Imogen was waiting for him at the door. Cool, slim fingers pressed his in a firm handshake. Billy gulped. In her high heels she was as tall as he was and wide-set eyes of limestone grey bored into his. She was in her early forties but with barely a wrinkle to show for it. Blonde, elegant and expensively clad in caramel cashmere, she was as immaculately groomed as a champion show-jumper. Billy fancied her rotten at once.
>
> *Lust on the Loose*, Noel Amos (1993)

Show not tell

This is also standard advice and ranks alongside being specific. Naturally it applies to the erotic writer – maybe it has even more significance in this genre. We've all arrived at the moment in a less-than-excellent thriller or action novel when the hero, taking time out from daring deeds, escorts his decorative dinner-date back to her place. After some repartee and a heavy-handed pass, they embrace. At which point the author writes: 'then an incredibly sensuous session of love-making followed.' End of chapter. And the reader feels cheated. The author has told us what happened but he has not shown us. Frankly, he might as well not have bothered.

It's unlikely you will make precisely this mistake, of course. You'll cut the macho stuff and go straight to the clinch on the sofa. However, you might pay lip service to events before the heavy breathing and say something like: 'Yvette proved to be a most charming dinner companion, witty and intelligent as well as beautiful. The evening flew by as if on wings.' Oh really? This won't do. You have to demonstrate the wit and intelligence because the reader won't take it on trust. Far better to send your lovers straight to bed without anything to eat at all.

Similarly, when the two dinner companions climb between the sheets, you cannot say: 'Victor was a wonderful lover, virile and powerful, yet sensitive to her needs. He did things to her she had never experienced before, raising her to peaks of ecstasy beyond her wildest dreams.' You might be able to get away with this kind of writing in steamy romances where the veil of vague generality still cloaks the lovers from the reader's curious eye. Not here, though. The veil belongs on the carpet next to the Yvette's discarded knickers.

You've got to put the reader right next to the bed and give him a grandstand view while Victor *shows* how virile, powerful, sensitive, etc. he is. So, the reader will be watching as Victor bends to caress the pale pink nubs of Yvette's nipples, he'll see Yvette shiver at the touch of her lover's lips on her aroused flesh, he'll hear the catch of indrawn breath in her throat as Victor nips a pert bud between his teeth, he'll feel the heat rising from their naked bodies as Victor sinks to place his lips on the pale fleece between her legs, he'll taste the honey of her excitement as Victor begins to kiss her sex, the scent of her in his nostrils – and, when a sudden orgasm shakes her whole body like a leaf in a storm, the reader will know she doesn't care a fig that she's just betrayed her husband yet again.

The reader should experience what goes on as vividly as you can convey it. It helps to cater to all the senses – sight, sound, touch, taste and smell (though maybe not in such a contrived fashion as above) – and also to let the reader know what your characters are feeling.

The facts of the matter are that show-not-tell goes to the heart of writing fiction of whatever nature. Novelists do more than tell their story, they try to bring it to life.

Tenses

The overwhelming majority of commercial novels are told in the past tense. The novelist is relating events that have already taken place and so it is natural to write in this way. There are exceptions, of course. Sometimes a special book comes along – Scott Turow's

Presumed Innocent, for example – and its impact is enhanced by the use of the present tense.

The present tense can also be effective in conveying sexual desire, as here:

> In my heart I know she isn't a virgin, but perhaps childless with pink buds for nipples or even if they're sucked and dark I don't mind. Wears a green scarf around her nice neck. Necks should be white and long with a blue nervous vein twitching with the nervousness of life in general. My good gracious saviour, she's looking over here. Hide? What am I? A scoundrel, a sneak? Not a bit. Face her. You're lovely. Absolutely lovely. Put my face on your spring breasts. Take you to Paris and tie your hair in knots with summer leaves.
>
> *The Ginger Man,* J. P. Donleavy (1955)

The advantages of the present tense are its immediacy, its now-ness. Events that have taken place are given more punch by the pretence that they are happening right now, as you read the words on the page.

In short bursts this can make a powerful grab for the reader's attention – which is why publisher's cover copy is written in the present though the novel inside has been composed in the past. But to sustain a long narrative in the present requires considerable skill. Try it for yourself. Afterwards, I bet you'll slip back into the past with the relief of someone putting on old shoes after a day spent in an unyielding new pair.

If you like the effect of the present tense it's worth noting that it is possible to combine both past and present in one narrative. The most likely way of doing this is to tell the bulk of the story in the past and then to switch to the present for those vivid moments you wish to highlight. *The Ginger Man,* from which I have just quoted, is written in this way and there are many other novels that change tense throughout their course. There are examples in erotica, too.

It begins now.

And it's pure and utter bliss.

With practised skill the unseen, unknown man takes command and I can do nothing more than lie there whimpering on the end of his cock as he rides me firmly and masterfully to a shattering conclusion. My submission is total. He delivers me to such a climax that all the pent-up tension and apprehension I'd felt before floods out of me in a great wave of ecstasy. The power of it overwhelms me completely, leaves me clinging to the couch like a shipwrecked mariner washed up after a storm.

The Pleasure Ring, Kitt Gerrard (1997)

Adjectives, adverbs, etc.

If you read erotica you'll be familiar with the style of the following:

He put his big thick rock-hard cock deeply into her warm wet welcoming pussy and low gurgling moans came softly from her full lush red mouth as his large strong questing fingers greedily reached for her huge swollen strawberry-crested tits.

This is not easy to read, I'm sure you'll agree, unless the reader is so deprived of stimulation that all critical faculties have gone out of the window. There are too many adjectives – it's as if the author is trying to make the word count on adjectives alone – every verb has an adverb and, as a result, the sentence is too long.

What happens if we prune the adjectives a bit?

He put his thick cock deeply into her wet pussy and low moans came softly from her lush mouth as his strong

> fingers greedily reached for her strawberry-crested tits.

That's easier to assimilate, I'd say, but still flat and boring. How about:

> He thrust his cock into her warm, wet pussy and her lush lips parted in a moan as his fingers ransacked her strawberry-tipped breasts.

Now at least we've got a workman-like sentence. I have:
1. restricted the adjectives
2. changed the passive to the active in 'her lips parted in a moan'
3. combined 'greedily reached' into 'ransacked'
4. changed 'strawberry-crested tits' to 'strawberry-tipped breasts'.

Here are the reasons I've done these things:

1. Since most of the adjectives had to go, I've focused on the woman. In general, you can't go wrong by describing the principle lust object in a book and since, in my mind anyway, this is a 'man's' book I've kept the emphasis on the woman. If this were a 'woman's' book we probably wouldn't start from here, as they say, but you could put the emphasis on the man. It might come out something like this: He thrust his erect phallus into her sex and she moaned as his cruel fingers plundered her tender breasts.

2. I prefer the active to the passive form, it's more direct, less confusing and makes for stronger prose. I didn't choose the most direct form here – 'she moaned as his fingers, etc.' – because I wanted to maintain the focus on her and include the phrase 'lush lips'.

3. A descriptive verb like 'ransack' does a lot of work in a sentence. It combines the verb and the adverb of 'greedily reached' and is thus stronger and more concise. The meaning is slightly altered, I admit, but I prefer the new one.

4. On reflection, the combination of 'crested' and 'tits' brought to mind small birds rather than mouth-watering mammaries. And if I'd altered it to 'strawberry-tipped tits' I would have exchanged the fluttering wildlife for a piece of alliteration – 'tipped tits' – that sounded clumsy to my ear. It would also have reverberated with 'lush lips' in the previous clause.

After all that, I make no claims for the finished sentence in question – it probably ought to be two sentences, in any case, with the break coming after 'pussy'. However, if you have stayed with me this long, the points to remember are:

1. Keep control of the adjectives, don't blanket-cover your nouns.
2. Choose the active over the passive.
3. Choose descriptive verbs and cut down on adverbs where you can.
4. Listen to the sound of the words in your head (reading your prose out loud can help).

Modifiers

> Generally speaking, Ralph was somewhat slow on the uptake if a woman showed a possible interest in him. For the most part he never noticed sideways glances and the fairly unnecessary touch on the arm. But when Gwen, a quite good-looking redhead who'd had rather a lot to drink, let her hand come to rest on his thigh beneath the table, her intent was pretty obvious even to him. And when her fingers crept higher, till they were nearly touching his cock, he was almost speechless with desire.

What do these 'rathers' and 'quites' and 'almosts' signify? Individually they have a meaning and can't be objected to. Collectively, they rob sentences of their clarity. Reading prose of this kind is like walking across a muddy field and at each step collecting another clod on your boots. You soon get bogged down.

The overall effect of an author hedging bets so consistently is to clog up the text. If you find yourself qualifying every statement, be brave and try stripping the offending words out. You may feel the need to reinstate one or two later but my guess is you'll end up with stronger, leaner, faster prose. A revised version of the paragraph above might read like this:

> Ralph was slow on the uptake if a woman showed an interest in him. He never noticed sideways glances and the light, unnecessary, touch on his arm. But when Gwen, a good-looking redhead who'd had a lot to drink, let her hand come to rest on his thigh beneath the table, her intent was obvious even to him. And when her fingers crept higher, till they were touching his cock, he was speechless with desire.

However, note that the modifier issue is more tricky in non-fiction when the writer is dealing with nuances of the truth. In fiction, after all, the truth is entirely in your hands.

Dialogue

The function of dialogue in erotica is no different to its job elsewhere. It's an interesting topic that is covered in detail in many places. Here's a resumé of the received wisdom.

1. There has to be a point

Speech in a novel bears little relation to speech in the real world. If you're skilful it may appear to be entirely natural. In practice it will be formalised shorthand, presenting information and advancing the action in a conversational form. So, no padding. No filling up the pages with irrelevant interchanges. Look at every passage of conversation and ask yourself, 'What's the point of this bit?'

2. The reader has to know who's speaking

This is relatively easy in a two-handed conversation where the occasional 'she said' or mention of the other party's name will make it clear. When three or more are involved, however, you must work harder. It must be obvious, either by direct attribution or by inference, exactly who is speaking at any one time.

3. Resist fancy attributions

There's nothing wrong with frequent repetition of 'he said' and 'she said'. The reader will probably not notice the repetition at all. What will be noticed is 'Simon interpolated', 'Charlotte interjected', 'Sarah chirped', etc. Dialogue that is stuffed full of elaborate attributions is thoroughly irritating to read and indicates 'amateur at work'.

Similarly, adverbial attributions are a menace:

'Is that a pistol in your pocket?' she said provocatively.

'You are truly beautiful,' he said reverently.

'So God's gift to women is back in town,' she said sarcastically.

In all these instances the adverb is redundant. Either the spoken words are provocative, reverent, sarcastic or they are not – sticking an adverbial label next to the attribution won't alter the case.

4. Keep dialect to a minimum

If one of your characters has a pronounced accent and you wish to indicate to the reader exactly how his or her speech sounds there's no need to spell it phonetically throughout. The last thing a reader wants is to have to decipher the indecipherable when the pace is hotting up. Make it clear at once your character has a distinct speech style, for example by way of another's reaction, and then leave it at that.

'You are a very beautiful woman,' Philippe said.

Marianne sipped her brandy and rested her head on the side of the bath. 'Tell me more,' she said and closed her eyes.

The alcohol and the warm water made her drowsy. The Frenchman's wonderful voice ravished her senses like an orchestra in full flow.

> *Yoo are a vair byootiful wooman. I wursheep yore boday...*
>
> Men had said these things to her before but not in fractured English with all the intensity of a Jacques Brel song.
>
> *Lust Under Licence*, Noel Amos (1995)

Thereafter Philippe can speak normally, with just the odd *mot français* thrown in to remind us of his origins.

5. Beware of conversational throat-clearing. Which is:

'Oh, Shelley!'

'Oh, hi, Candice. What happened last night?'

'Well, Brad took me out for dinner. And a moonlight drive in his Mercedes.'

'Mmm, lucky you. Did he get you in the back seat?'

'Er... I don't want to get into that.'

'Oh, come on. I want to know what happened.'

'Well... you won't tell Dave, will you?'

'Hey, what do you take me for?'

'Um, OK, then. I'm just dying to talk about it.'

And so on.

Irritating, isn't it? This writer's characters can't open their mouths without clearing their throats. Each remark is prefaced with 'oh', 'well', 'er', 'um' and similar noises. The first word in every line above can be removed without changing the sense one iota. It's easy to fall into this habit. Many people speak this way and, by unconsciously aping it, the words seem to flow on to the page. Once you're aware of the tendency it's easy to correct.

Wandering body parts

'In the smoky gloom of the party, his eyes followed her around the room' – I once had a schoolteacher who was particularly sarcastic about this kind of grammatical slip-up. 'And I suppose they followed her down the road and on to the number nineteen bus, you fool.' 'But you know what I *mean*, sir,' I protested at the time.

I wonder what that teacher might make of the erotic equivalent. I've just come across this example, whose author shall remain anonymous:

> Her nipples, loading themselves with blood, attempted to torpedo their way out of her jumper.

The same goes for this, also authentic, sample:

> Her breasts looked as if they rode free on the rhythm, her hips leading them into their motion.

In erotic writing, parts of the body have a tendency to develop minds of their own. It is most important that you keep track of them, otherwise you'll be in trouble when you get to the orgy scenes.

> Two pear-shaped breasts thrust out, the right one within easy cupping reach of the hand on his arm surrounding her waist, while the blond stud was being fed the nipples of the redhead whose mouth was being stretched wide by a monstrously thick prick...

When three or four or more are gathered together in chapter fifteen with all sinews straining and the mercury about to shoot off the temperature gauge, someone has got to keep a cool head. That someone is you. You must know what goes where and who it belongs to. Make a diagram, use dolls or, if you're very persuasive, get people to pose for you – but somehow visualise events so that your characters do not attempt the anatomically impossible. Otherwise, by the time the reader has stopped to work out that the penis invading Corinne is owned by Greg not John then his enthusiasm for your climactic encounter will be long gone.

Repetition

This is one of the pitfalls of the genre, both in the sense of the erotic activity you describe and the language you use. With luck, your stylistic tics will become obvious to you on rereading your own work. Every writer has a tendency to favour certain means of expression and experienced ones learn to keep their habits in check. This requires an analytic eye and a cool head – which you may not possess when gripped by a frenzy of erotic creativity.

It is irritating to a reader to come across the same pet phrase time after time. 'The living silk of her skin', 'a cock as rigid as a guardsman', 'her breasts undulating like waves' – these images may work well the first time around but will lose their effect on each repetition. Once the reader notices them, the novelist's spell is broken.

Similarly you should be aware of your own sexual preferences. If your favourite fantasy is to watch a six-foot blonde putting on black silk stockings then write the scene once, in full technicolour, and resist the impulse to return to it. And if you must have another stocking-donning scene then be cunning and ring the changes so it is not obvious. Sex fantasies are repetitive (the sex act itself is repetitive – ask any married couple) but your job is to turn a two-minute pop song into a symphony of limitless variation without losing any of its instant appeal.

Be your own editor

There's nothing like having someone else read your book with a critical eye. They will always spot something you've missed. Nevertheless, you should aim to present your work in as polished a state as you can manage. When you lurch from your desk at the end of Chapter 15, with the last ecstatic cries from Castle Climax still echoing in your ears, don't imagine that your job is finished. Celebrate in an appropriate manner certainly. Take a break from your labours and, if you are able, forget the whole thing for a few days. Then sit down with your typescript, pencil in hand and read your novel through as carefully as you can.

On a separate piece of paper make notes of things you must double-check. How do you spell Dolce & Gabbana? If your heroine, on a spree with her lover in Rome, rings her husband on a business trip in Chicago, how come they're both about to go out for the evening? And, when you've sorted out the time difference, are you sure the opera house where the wife spends her evening is called La Scala?

Don't rely on the editor or copy-editor to fix these things. There's no guarantee they will and if they do they won't think any better of you for not correcting it in the first place. Be your own editor and get it as right as you can before submission.

> 'The most essential gift for a good writer is a built-in shock-proof shit-detector.'
>
> Ernest Hemingway

Your turn

Conjure up the image of someone desirable in your mind – preferably someone you think of as 'lovely' or 'handsome' or 'beautiful'. It could be a person you know well or one you've never met, like a movie star. Describe them in a short paragraph and try to convey the essence of what makes them special. Look carefully at what you've written. Is it full of phrases that don't have a precise meaning – 'dazzling smile', 'incredible eyes', 'fabulous breasts'? If so, think hard about each group of words. What makes his smile 'dazzling'? Is it because his grin is slightly lopsided? Or because he laughs with his eyes as well as his mouth? Or because he smiles so rarely? If so, say so. Discard the easy, top-of-the-head clichés in favour of the specific.

> They met in the bar. Jill was witty, Bill was
> flirtatious and by nine o'clock they were heading
> home to bed.

Write the scene so readers can see for themselves the witty,
flirty behaviour.

Analyse a page or two of your own writing.

If it's written in the past tense, try changing into the
present all the way through. Compare the two versions.
Does the present gain anything over the past? How easy
was it to do without slipping back unconsciously into the
past tense?

Delete all the adjectives and adverbs. Does this stripped-
down version still work?

What has it lost and what has it gained, in your opinion?

Put back only those adjectives and adverbs that you feel
are essential. Do you prefer the old version or this new one?

Examine your pages for words that modify your meaning –
'almost', 'nearly', 'generally', etc. Try taking them out and
see if that strengthens your prose. Are all these qualifications necessary? Make sure you're not just hedging your
bets.

Take a passage of dialogue, from your own work or from
another writer. How does the sequence move the situation
forward?

Is it always clear who's speaking?

Look out for fancy attributions and irrelevant adverbs.

Also, beware throat-clearing.

Subject an orgy scene – one of your own maybe – to a
similar analysis. Has the author created a clear picture of
who is doing what to whom?

8

GENRES WITHIN THE GENRE

> 'In erotica, more than in any other genre, success is in the mind of the reader – one man's wildly stimulating encounter is another's squalid pantomime.'
>
> J.-P. Spencer

Contrary to a widely held opinion that erotic novels are 'all the same', the garden of erotica is fertile ground for many different blooms. Here are some of the varieties that flourish within the mainstream.

For women

The most significant development in erotic publishing in recent years has been the arrival of lists aimed specifically at a female readership. Virgin Publishing's Black Lace is the pioneer. Launched in 1993 and backed by a promotional campaign that in itself was an innovation – no publisher had ever spent a marketing bean on erotica until that point – it has become synonymous with the phrase 'women's erotica'. Its success has focused media attention on this area of publishing, undeniably altering public perception of erotica in general. If it's OK for women to read dirty books, runs the thinking, then maybe they're not so dirty after all. As a result, women's erotica has legitimised the market and has established a significant presence on the shelves.

'It's very important to me that the female characters are strong independent women. Before women's erotic novels the only kind of literature involved 'shrinking violets' in Mills & Boon novels or women with no brain or self-respect in porno magazines. Women's erotic novels are a breath of fresh air.'

Female respondent to sex survey

Without digressing into the dangerous currents of sexual politics, it is obvious that women's lives have changed radically in recent decades. Now women can control their reproductive cycles, have careers, earn money and exist independently of men if they choose. Inevitably this independence is reflected in their sexuality.

'Masturbation for women was such a taboo that in 1966 surveys on the subject, only 18% of women admitted doing it. In 1992 that number had jumped to 80%. And, as Dr Jocelyn Elders, former US Surgeon General, says, "Probably the rest lie."

Cosmopolitan

In erotica from previous eras, the story is often told from a woman's point-of-view – usually of an innocent-turned-whore who fornicates with the appetite of a male – but written by a man. Nowadays it is as likely that women will be doing the writing. In contemporary erotica, it is recognised that women have sexual needs as significant as men's and that they can control their own erotic destiny. The female protagonists need no longer be whores or rich nymphomaniacs, they can be politicians, mistresses of industry, soldiers – any damn thing they please, in fact. This is a welcome development for all erotic writers and its effects are not confined to the female lists.

What distinguishes women's erotica from men's?

In many respects, not much. The most significant difference is that this is an area off-limits to men – as creators, that is. No one knows how many men read the books that proudly proclaim that here is 'erotic fiction written by women for women' though it is fair to say that a line like this is guaranteed to pique male curiosity. However, if you are a man with aspirations to write for Black Lace or its sister lists you are out of luck – you are barred by reason of your gender.

The assumption is that men write about sex differently to women: That they are obsessed with female bodies – the tits, the cunt, the ass – at the expense of feeling; that they conceive love-making in terms of conquest and possession; that the sensual accompaniments to an erotic moment – the scent of honeysuckle on the breeze, the moonlight on the water, the strains of a distant dance band as the lovers embrace (I'm exaggerating but you get the picture) – are not important to them. In other words, men are uncouth gluttons with eyes on the cheesecake even as they scoff the burger and fries. Women, on the other hand, are the true sensual gourmets with a style and a language capable of far greater subtlety.

> 'At the time we were all writing erotica at a dollar a page, I realised that for centuries we had had only one model for this literary genre – the writing of men. I was already conscious of a difference between the masculine and feminine treatment of sexual experience. I knew that there was a great disparity between Henry Miller's explicitness and my ambiguities – between his humorous, Rabelaisian view of sex and my poetic descriptions of sexual relationships... I had a feeling that Pandora's box contained the mysteries of women's sensuality, so different from man's and for which man's language was inadequate.'
>
> Anaïs Nin, Preface to *Delta of Venus*,
> (1940/1, published 1969)

Anaïs Nin, with her emphasis on feelings and poetic expression, is the acknowledged guru of this style, which is as much a reaction to the crudity of some male writing as a distinctive voice of its own. Hence, in contemporary women's erotica, the pages are not splattered with Anglo-Saxon vocabulary and the words employed for sex are softer:

ten-inch cocks don't ram themselves into sopping cunts – instead golden phalluses pulse within tingling quims. The most basic terms like 'fuck' and 'cunt' are restricted in their use, the latter being avoided completely by some lists. The sexual activities that are described, however, are as varied and exhausting as can be found elsewhere.

> Marisa bit on her soft lower lip as she watched them, her body quickening with desire. They were all eagerly pleasuring one another, heedless of the rest of the company. Tom was showing the flushed spinster, Emily, how to lick his cock, while John was making the church-warden's wife masturbate him. She was eagerly rubbing his foreskin up and down while he whispered rude words in her ear. Caleb, meanwhile, was keeping his two women happy with amazing vigour. Lucy was already flushed and breathless with the pleasure of his big, skilful tongue lapping hungrily at her secret parts, while Hannah was lifting herself high on the thick, throbbing stem of his penis then pounding down again, rubbing voraciously at her own clitoris as her fierce orgasm started to envelop her.
>
> *Ace of Hearts*, Lisette Allen (1996)

In books for women, most of the action is seen from the point of view of the female protagonist though occasionally an author may offer a third-person insight into a male character. The heroines are young women who, no matter how innocent they may be at the beginning of the novel, have a curiosity about their sexuality and the spirit to take control of it. Quite often they begin as experienced sexual adventurers who, in the course of the narrative, seduce new lovers much as male protagonists have traditionally done. These ladies have omnivorous sexual tastes that are not necessarily restricted to the opposite sex. The heroine will make love to a secondary female character, a friend or servant, in an uninhibited fashion that has no parallel – at the moment, at least – in books for heterosexual men.

Samoya grabbed Irene's hand and pushed her on to the bed. 'Let's lie head to tail.'

She slid her hands down over Irene's body and clasped her breasts then slowly flattened herself and moved further down so that her slave's pale fringed sex was exposed. Samoya placed a finger at its tip and gently began to caress it. Irene opened beneath her fingers and her breath came in quick-fire gasps. The two of them moved sideways together and laid their mouths and tongues upon each other's sex, working fast upon one another until their juices spread out over their legs, their bellies tightened into a ball and they came in tandem.

Handmaiden of Palmyra, Fleur Reynolds (1994)

Handmaiden of Palmyra is set in third-century Syria, which indicates another departure for this style of novel. Though the present-day predominates, settings can range throughout history, providing unusual and atmospheric surroundings. It is perceived that women like the detail of exotic scene-setting – particularly in descriptions of clothes. In a genre in which sexually aroused young women are required to dress and undress on a regular basis, there's a lot of scope for the inventive novelist to indulge in sensual descriptions of period attire.

Her white silk tunic, split down the front, fell at her feet. Under it she wore a breast halter made of tiny jewelled chains. A deep belt of gold leather cinched her waist. More chains were secured to the centre of the belt; they trailed over but did not obscure her fleece – displayed prominently as always. Loose, open-fronted trousers of white silk clothed her legs and were drawn in tightly at each ankle. Leyla had dressed her with special care for this meeting. She knew she looked her sensual best.

The Captive Flesh, Cleo Cordell (1993)

There's no room for wimps – male or female – in women's erotica. The leading males tend towards the domineering and sadistic, so too, many of the secondary female characters. But despite the spirited nature of the heroines, the men are frequently successful in bending them to their will. Often the female protagonist is made captive and subjected to a parade of lascivious sexual torments. Whips, chains, handcuffs and other instruments of torture may be used in the drama of domination and submission, so too more imaginative props.

Fiona tightened her legs on the rocking horse and she heaved her body back a little. Immediately the knob on the end of the cunningly situated saddle-horn was pulled back too and moved nearer to the front of her vagina, pressing against the top surface of her moist sheath. At the same time her breasts moved and the rubber gripped her closely making her throw back her head as the sparks of pleasure shot through the burgeoning flesh.

'Faster,' said Alessandro dispassionately, and now Fiona began to ride like one possessed, terrified of where the crop might fall if she disobeyed...

Fiona's Fate, Frederica Alleyn (1994)

The key to this kind of writing – as in all erotica – is to invent a world in which your readers have permission to explore all their sexual desires, particularly those they would shrink from putting into practice.

If you want to try your hand at a woman's erotic novel, you should:

1. be a woman yourself
2. use the third-person, from a predominately female viewpoint
3. create an adventurous heroine
4. adopt the softer language of the sub-genre
5. use it to describe detailed and inventive sex
6. create a setting with scope for atmospheric description, especially of clothes.

SM

> 'The relation of love to pain is one of the most difficult problems, and yet one of the most fundamental, in the whole range of sexual psychology. Why is it that love inflicts, and even seeks to inflict, pain? Why is it that love suffers pain, and even seeks to suffer it?'
>
> Havelock Ellis

SM stands for sadomasochism, a word coined by Freud and derived from the names of the Marquis de Sade and the author of *Venus in Furs*, Leopold von Sacher-Masoch. The term is a useful shorthand to cover that whole sphere of sexual activity in which suffering is ritually traded to the satisfaction of the giver and the receiver.

At the root of SM lies a relationship between two people, not necessarily of the opposite sex, which depends on a trade-off of pain for pleasure. The psychology of submission and domination, the ritual of punishment and the heightened sensual awareness that accompanies it, is endlessly adaptable and highly dramatic. Devotees of SM will create a scenario in which the receiver is at the mercy of the giver but in reality permission will have been granted by the former to the latter. This element of role-playing and the exercise of the imagination involved is tailor-made for the erotic novelist.

SM scenes and situations are employed in almost all forms of erotica, Often in a mild manner, as a side dish to the main course. The cruel master, the black-basqued mistress, the cowed slave, the young maid whose spirit must be tamed – these and many more are recognisable characters in erotic novels. So too the apparatus of SM – the canes, paddles, ropes, collars and all the many instruments of punishment and restraint – furnishes countless erotic narratives. It is perfectly possible to write sexy books without reference to SM yet its influence is pervasive and, on some publishers' lists, exclusive.

In all probability, if this is the kind of novel that you want to write then you will already be well-versed in its literary heritage and the books that are currently available. There exists a library of Victorian and Edwardian literature devoted to flagellation stories – see the reading list that follows this chapter. The key text for the modern reader, however, must be *The Story of O* in which a young woman voluntarily becomes the sex slave of her lover and his friends. The novel is a journey of sensual self-awareness that makes its mark on all who read it, as the heroine graduates from mild submission to the whims of her first lover, René, to branding and mutilation on the orders of a new master, Sir Stephen. The paradox is that the end product of this cruelty is ecstasy.

> Objectively now, what was René next to Sir Stephen? Threads of paper, strings of straw – such in actual truth were the ties whereby he had bound her to him, and which he had so quickly severed; and that quick, that easy sunderance was what those so-frail ties symbolised. Whereas what peaceful security, what reassurance, what delight, this iron ring which pierces flesh and weighs eternally, this mark that will remain forever, the master's hand which lays you down to rest on a couch of rock, the love of a master who is capable of pitilessly appropriating unto himself that which he loves. And, by way of final conclusion, O told herself that she had only loved René as a means for learning of love and for finding out how to give herself better, as a slave, as an ecstatic slave, to Sir Stephen.
>
> *The Story of O*, Pauline Réage (1954)

In practice, much modern SM is less intellectual and more in-your-face than this elegant French fable.

> I think that my Master must have given me at least a hundred strokes with his hard whip. My bottom was on fire and my body was jerking and quivering in lovely pain. I wanted it to go on forever. The stroke of the whip on the bare bum is nothing less than ecstasy. The strokes of my Master's whip made my cunt wetter and wetter

> until, I suppose at the hundredth stroke, my belly
> shivered in her heat, and I came to a spend.
>
> *The Governess Abroad*, Yolande Celbridge (1996)

If this style of erotica is for you, then you probably don't need
reminding that:

1 'accidental' pain is not required, only that which is deliberately
   inflicted
2 the ritual of punishment is essential
3 pain and pleasure are two sides of the same coin
4 physical submission is a means to mental submission.

Gay erotica

> 'Each word of a work of gay erotica is a spear for the eyes or
> groin or gut or heart of straight society. Make every word as
> sharp as you can.'
>
> Lars Eighner

As well as shelves designated for erotica, these days high street bookshops are likely also to have an area set aside for gay books – indeed
this section was probably established first. Gay erotica straddles both
these ghettos. It's the kind of labelling that writers abhor but which
publishers and booksellers accept as inevitable. Nobody likes to be put
in a box but if that box has a prominent place in the store and shouts
loudly to the target reader 'Over here!' then the author would be well-
advised to swallow any objections.

In the gay ghetto can be found all kinds of offerings, from the literary
novels of Alan Hollingshurst and Jeanette Winterson to gay travel
guides to photographic art books. There you will also find the gay
equivalent of the novels we have been discussing, most of them
published by the Badboy imprint of Masquerade Books in New York.

Though there are many similarities between gay and straight erotic
writing – principally in the shared intention to excite the reader

sexually – there are also differences beyond the obvious. The words above, taken from Eighner's highly commended *Elements of Arousal: How to write and sell gay men's erotica* (1994), illustrate one of them. Gay writing of whatever nature has a political context. Writers like Eighner have a pride in their work and want it to count for something beyond giving a satisfying reading experience. Here's another voice, Paul Reed, who writes as Max Exander.

> 'Pornography, including SM fiction, is an expression of larger goals: the fusion of body and spirit, the triumph of liberty over conformity, the understanding that sex and sexuality in all stripes is an integral part of being fully human and is not shameful. It is an affirmation of lifestyle, or dreams made real, of raw feelings and desires made manifest, no longer hidden in the shadows, no longer disallowed.'
>
> From the Introduction to *Leathersex*, Max Exander (1994)

As for the content of the books themselves, in many of them SM action abounds in which tops – the topmen, the masters, the pain-givers – bend the bottoms – the inferiors, the slaves, the receivers – to their will. Here are drill sergeants initiating recruits, leather-clad bikers terrorising curious students, heavy-handed cops laying down the law to teenage miscreants and so on. Though to generalise is odious, gay men's erotica is, in many respects, the mirror-image of female erotic fiction. It glories in conquest and domination, in an obsessive focus on body parts and keeping score; softness and sensitivity in language and feeling are not obvious. Nevertheless, beyond the theatrical images of cruelty, there is intense emotion:

> I knelt in communion with Mr Benson like a religious fanatic who had journeyed to a shrine. My week of abstinence, my humiliation, my trial, had all been for this. This godstick and these ripe and full nuts hanging beneath my chin. I went mad with desire for his cock. Oblivious to my branded butt, I chowed down on the pole in front of me.

> Mr Benson's cock.
>
> His fabled virility poked down my throat. I worked my head and neck to feel his smooth surface against my inside. Before long, his shaft began to swell with come. The veins pushed against the outer layer of skin. I gulped further down at the early warning and, when he shot, the precious juice pistolled straight into me, hardly any of it even into my mouth, the taste of this man – I can say it now – went straight to my soul!
>
> *Mr Benson*, John Preston (1992)

Specifically lesbian erotica is also available, though only the US has mass-market lists that are dedicated to it, principally the Masquerade imprint, Rosebud. These books are also SM-inclined, with an emphasis on sub-dom relationships. In the UK, with the exception of one-off anthologies for mainstream lists, there is little aimed at a specifically lesbian readership from the regular publishers of erotica. This is despite the fact that lesbian scenes are commonly offered in hetero erotica. At present, publishers clearly don't see a big enough market. My guess is that this will change over the next few years and, just as we are now beginning to see UK-originated erotica for gay men, the equivalent for gay women will follow. If this is an area you think you could exploit, I'd suggest you keep your ideas on the back-burner and watch developments.

Another noticeable feature of gay erotica – for both a male and female audience – is the proliferation of the short story. Anthologies abound, some of them from major publishers and on mainstream lists. This doubtless has a lot to do with the current state of the magazine market in the US – where many of these tales first appeared. It's worth noting that there's a better chance of seeing a gay story in print than a straight one – provided you can research your target outlets. The advice here is, get your hands on magazines that are current. If they publish fiction, note the nature of the stories and the length. Send submissions to the editor as listed on the masthead and enclose postage for return. Keep a record, build a dossier of names and addresses, and persevere. You'll end up with better knowledge of the market – and better contacts – than I could give you here. Good luck.

Fetish sub-genres

These are books which cater to obsessive interest in certain items of clothing – rubber and leather-ware, high heels, silk and satin, fur, and so on. These novels may also explore the potential of less obviously erotic areas of the body – the foot for example, as in this extract:

> As his penis repeatedly slid forward to twitch and jolt in the daintily pointed toe of the fairy shoe, Prince Steven could not shake the notion that he was making love to the masked princess herself. Somehow the shoe was part of her and he made love to it reverently. His mind reeled, recalling the vision of her prettily arched feet, the coy impudence of her silk-stockinged toes, the rounded sensual curve of her pretty heels and the maddening shape of her calves and ankles.
>
> *Sinderella*, Anonymous (Titian Beresford) (1993)

If this kind of minority interest reflects your own concerns I suspect it will emerge naturally in your writing. In which case, don't suppress it – it may well make your work more distinctive. As yet, I'm aware of no mass-market list founded on such specific matters of taste, though individual titles do crop up within erotic imprints and doubtless their afficionados sniff them out.

Science fiction and fantasy

'Aliens ain't sexy.'

Carl K. Mariner

In my experience, science fiction settings for erotic novels are rarely the basis for commercial success, which is a pity because these are often books where the author's imagination matches his or her talent for titillation. As a result, there is not much erotic SF being published at present and no UK lists make a point of asking for it. In the US, where there is a tradition of erotic science fiction publishing, the situation is healthier. Since the sixties, some of the best SF writers have turned their hand to erotica, including Philip Jose Farmer, Samuel Delany, Andrew Offutt and Charles Platt. But aesthetically satisfying though their efforts may be – to the extent that a loyal and indefatigable SF readership will take pains to seek them out – there is no sign of a significant market for erotica with a science fiction background.

One of the challenges the genre poses is to make technology titillating, as in this attempt:

> Tina held the box between her thighs, holding it there in front of her sex, poised. It began to move, to open, a weird, inorganic flower about to bloom. Planes of black plastic moved apart and from within the heart there emerged a point, a salient, expanding phallically towards her shaven sex. It was a flower, the petals opening like an iris, touching her pussy lips and opening them in turn. There was a moment when Tina's sex was open and visible, the glistening folds of flesh wet and pink and then the black flower shrivelled back and a bulbous glans pushed softly into her body. She sighed loudly, almost an expression of pleasant surprise, and the thing was inside her.
>
> 'This is *sooo gooood...*' she whispered.
>
> *Desire*, Robert Arden (1995)

In the survey Delta conducted on readers' preferences, science fiction was the least favoured of all settings. My theory is that readers who don't like science fiction at any price won't be seduced by sexy content, while regular SF fans are averse to hybrid versions and will look beyond the genre for their erotic reading. It would be encouraging to see this situation change but don't count it.

Horror and supernatural

The same situation as above applies here, with the exception of the sub-sub-genre of vampire erotica. Inspired by the Hammer House of Horror and the novels of Anne Rice (who has also written fantasy SM as A. M. Roquelaure), the sexy vampire has almost become a stock character in erotica. You don't need to reach for Freud to see the erotic possibilities of a scenario that contains blood-sucking, glistening fangs, immortality and the heaving cleavage of Ingrid Pitt. The most notable author is Valentina Cilescu with her *Kiss of Death* series, a multi-volume epic whose settings range from Ancient Egypt to the present-day House of Commons (which could explain a lot). This extract will give you the flavour:

> All Mara's white magic could not protect her now. For the Master was growing, his body expanding, swelling, deforming, until at last he towered high above her, filling the room, his evil eyes still fixing her with that fiery red gaze.
>
> And as she watched, unable to turn away for he still held her fast, she saw the Master's prick also begin to change its form, swelling, lengthening, growing beyond all belief until it became a parody of a penis – a prick as thick as a man's torso and as long as a limb.
>
> The Master's mouth opened and he began to speak, his voice hoarse and rasping, like the voice of a serpent turned into a cruel caricature of human form:
>
> 'Little slut.' he hissed, 'I have you now and I have you for ever. You cannot escape me.'
>
> *The Phallus of Osiris*, Valentina Cilescu (1993)

Most lists, I suspect, would not be averse to a vampire scenario, provided it were adapted to their requirements.

Selected reading

Women's erotica

Delta of Venus, Anaïs Nin (1940/1, published 1969)

The Captive Flesh, Cleo Cordell (1993)

Web of Desire, Sophie Danson (1993)

No Lady, Saskia Hope (1993)

Handmaiden of Palmyria, Fleur Reynolds (1994)

Fiona's Fate, Frederica Alleyn (1994)

A Private Affair, Carol Anderson (1995)

Voluptuous Voyage, Lacey Carlyle (1995)

SM

From the extensive body of Victorian and Edwardian flagellation texts:

Venus in Furs, Leopold von Sacher-Masoch (c.1860)

Gynecocracy, 'Julian Robinson' (1893)

A Man with a Maid, Anonymous (1895)

The Memoirs of Dolly Morton, Hugues Rebell (1899)

'Frank' and I, Hugues Rebell (1902)

More recently:

The Story of O, Pauline Réage (1954)

The English Governess, Miles Underwood (1960)

Claiming of Sleeping Beauty, A. N. Roquelaure (Anne Rice) (1987)

The Training Grounds, Sarah Veitch (1994)

The Academy, Arabella Knight (1995)

Gay men's erotica

Mr Benson, John Preston (1992)

Beast of Burden, Aaron Travis (1993)

Leathersex, Max Exander (1994)

Whispered in the Dark, Lars Eighner (1995)

Lesbian

Bad Habits, Lindsay Welsh (1992)

The Penguin Book of Lesbian Short Stories,
ed Margaret Reynolds (1994)

Mistress with a Maid trilogy, Valentina Cilescu (1996)

Dial 'L' for Loveless, Allison Tyler (1996)

Fetish

Nina Foxton, Titian Beresford (1991)

Miss High-heels, Alizarin Lake (1993)

Sinderella, Anonymous (Titian Beresford) (1993)

The Pleasure Ring, Kitt Gerrard (1997)

Midnight Tales of Torment, Kitt Gerrard (1997)

Science fiction and fantasy

Flesh, Philip Jose Farmer (1960)

Tides of Lust, Samuel R. Delany (1973)

Tara of the Twilight, Lin Carter (1979)

Penetrators of Time, Merlin Kaye (1980)

Wicked, Andrea Arven (1991)

Desire, Robert Arden (1995)

The Sex Files, Files 1–4, Mariner, Li, Desoto, Horowitz (1997)

Horror and supernatural

Frankenstein 69, Ed Martin (1969)

Interview with the Vampire, Anne Rice (1976)

Kiss of Death, Valentina Cilescu (1992), also the succeeding
volumes in the sequence: *The Phallus of Osiris* (1993), *Empire
of Lust* (1994), *Masque of Flesh* (1995), *Vixens of Night* (1997)

A Slave to His Kiss, Anastasia Dubois (1995)

Eternal Kiss, Anastasia Dubois (1996)

9

WHERE TO DRAW THE LINE

> 'Obscenity is whatever gives a judge an erection.'
>
> Anonymous

How far can you go?

It has been many years since a work of fiction has been prosecuted for obscenity in the United Kingdom – since 1976, I believe, when *Inside Linda Lovelace* was acquitted at the Central Criminal Court in London. And though the authorities have shown interest in explicit texts from time to time – I remember some civilised conversations with the police when W. H. Allen published Henry Miller's *Opus Pistorum* in 1984 – it would take a sea-change in public attitudes to bring about any similar actions. To mount a successful public prosecution against a novel requires an enormous commitment of time and money with a high risk of failure. Frankly, the authorities have better things to do and are far more likely to take interest in visual material – magazines, videos and (doubtless) pornography on the Internet – than in the kind of books we are discussing here.

This does not mean that publishers are free to publish whatever hardcore material you care to submit. Leaving aside whether or not they may wish to publish the most extreme material, there are constraints on how they publish in this category. It is important to publishers to keep booksellers happy. In general, booksellers tolerate erotica because their customers buy it. Their minds would quickly cease to be so broad if their customers began to complain instead.

Should certain practices be gleefully described in your novel and discovered on the shelves of a leading book chain by an irate browser, who then wrote to the chairman of the chain concerned (with copies to his MP and the local newspaper) then there would be Trouble. The book chain would moan to the publisher, books (and not just yours) would be withdrawn from sale, the editor would have his knuckles rapped (at least) and you'd be looking for a new publisher.

What then are the 'certain practices' you must avoid?

Children

Erotica is a playground for consenting adults only. The age of consent in the UK is currently sixteen (eighteen for gay men – unless, of course, they're in bed with a woman) and it may be higher in other parts of the world where your book may end up on sale. There's no point in protesting that we are sexual beings from the moment we are born or that half your daughter's class were pregnant at the age of fifteen. As far as erotic fiction is concerned, young people are as pure as driven snow until the morning of their sixteenth birthday. After that, to paraphrase Mae West, they can drift.

Joking apart, sex with children is not an amusing topic and any book-seller accused of offering material for sale that describes paedophile activity will be horrified. Booksellers trust publishers to screen out offensive content and, in turn, publishers trust their authors to abide by the rules and not involve them in unnecessary editing chores.

Rule number one in erotica is: No kids.

Animals

Though dogs, horses and other beasts feature in sexual daydreams – see Nancy Friday's collections of secret fantasies, *Men in Love*, *Women on Top* and *The Secret Garden* – bestiality is also a taboo subject area. The standard advice is to avoid any sexual by-play with animals.

Rule two: No dogs.

Necrophilia

This means a sexual interest in dead bodies. Erotica requires that you keep your lovers alive.

Rule three: No corpses.

Blood and coercion

This general area is more tricky and just how far you can travel will depend on the requirements of the individual publisher's list. A lot of material currently on sale describes activities that, were they to take place in reality, would land the perpetrators in court. The key word here is 'consensual'. It is doubtful, should real-life police officers liberate any of the sorely abused heroes and heroines of sado-masochistic erotica from their dungeons, that any of them would actually press charges. You should be guided by the degree of violence that exists in the books that are on sale. I would also recommend that you avoid the word 'rape'. In practice, much of the whacking and flogging in erotica is window-dressing – the real issue is the mind-game of domination and submission.

Rule four: No excessive violence (but let your publisher define excessive).

Drugs

Be careful how you handle scenes that include drug-taking. Though sniffing, snorting and general pill-popping are facts of life and grist to the entertainment mill, publishers are sensitive about such matters in the context of erotica. Don't, for example, have character A ply character B with dope in order to take sexual advantage of her.

Rule five: Handle drugs with care.

Incest

Another tricky area. Some Victorian pornography abounds in enthusiastic family fucking, which evidently had a special resonance for its readers – I like to think of it as waving two fingers at the notion of the sanctified Victorian family. These days, however, we take a more realistic view of incestuous behaviour. The practice is, of course, illegal.

Rule six: No incest.

Copyright

This is a minefield but one which, with a little forethought, you can navigate without too much difficulty. If all the words in your book are your own, then you own the copyright in the Work (as it is referred to in the publishing contract). If someone were to reproduce, word for word and without your agreement, the epic act of fornication on the London Underground that makes up Chapter 10 of your novel then your copyright would be infringed. More to the point, you cannot lift someone else's Chapter 10 without their agreement.

Rule seven: Don't copy someone else's work without obtaining permission.

Some related copyright points

Copyright now extends for seventy years from the end of the year in which the author dies. This means you are free to quote from Shakespeare, Milton, Fielding, Austen, Dickens, Wilde and so on – though it is hard to imagine why, in this genre, you should want to do so. Obviously you should check death dates of writers you are uncertain about.

It is generally accepted that copyright does not lie in an idea but in the way that idea is expressed. So, to extend the example above, suppose instead of lifting the text of A. N. Other's *Bonking on the Bakerloo*, you wrote your own version, using his idea but your words. In that instance, even though derivative, *Desire on the District* would be your original work. And if Other should bring an action against you, its success would depend on how much you had used his creation as a labour-saving device.

You would only infringe someone else's copyright by helping yourself to a significant portion of their work. However, in the case of a poem or song lyrics, that may not be much and it does depend on the context in which you quote. In works of non-fiction there are accepted guidelines that indicate how much material may be used for critical or review purposes, often referred to as 'fair dealing'. These indicate that you may extract up to 400 words or a series of extracts (none exceeding 300 words) totalling 800 words from a work of prose, and a total of forty lines from a poem provided that this does not comprise more than a quarter of the whole work. On this basis, provided that you credit the author and the title of the work, you need not seek separate permission.

As far as the erotic fiction writer is concerned, most of this is irrelevant. However, I'd offer one piece of advice – resist quoting song lyrics, no matter how short the intended extract. Tracing the copyright holder and negotiating a fee that does not exceed the advance you were paid to write the book in the first place, can be a frustrating experience. That said, music publishers have justification for defending their territory. There's no denying that even a few words taken from a hit lyric can have a powerful resonance for a mass audience who sang along, danced and made passionate love to the original song. This is just the kind of effect you'd like your novel to have. But, however much the idea appeals, attempting to clear the permissions can be a nightmare. Save yourself time and money by following rule eight: Don't quote from songs.

There's no copyright in a title. If you want to call your book *Gone With the Wind*, go ahead and type it on the title page of your manuscript. There are any number of reasons why that title may not survive to the published version. I guarantee, however, that when it appears under the title of *Come with the Wind* it won't be because your publisher feared a lawsuit from the Margaret Mitchell estate.

You may be worried that your idea will be stolen before it is published and smother your submission with copyright credits accordingly. In practice, this is one of the last things you should worry about. Editorial departments of publishing houses are staffed by people on the look-out for projects they can raise at acquisitions meetings – the forum at which buying decisions are made. If you've got a good idea the editor's first impulse is to bring it up at this meeting in a proprietorial fashion and not to rip it off. If it finds favour then the editor will champion the project all the way through the publishing process. I've never heard of a good idea being turned down so the editor could write it herself. If she likes it, she'll want you to undertake the slog of writing it and she'll bask in the reflected glory of its success.

Libel

A libel is a defamatory statement published about a living person or a trading company. This is potentially the biggest legal booby-trap lying in wait for an erotic novelist. I know of one writer who likes to give his characters the names of people he's acquainted with. This is on the grounds that, should Miss X emerge from the woodwork and claim her reputation has been damaged, the author can claim he had another Miss X in mind all along and so the allegation can't be true. This seems to me an unnecessarily cautious way of proceeding.

At the other extreme, it goes without saying that you should not knowingly place a recognisable character in a situation that is liable to lower him or her in the estimation of others. No matter how much you dislike your former fiancée it would be folly to have her entertain the four-man staff of the post room between the black silk sheets you remember so well at 12, Bedside Villas. Quite apart from the pain her current fiancé might inflict on your person, the damage inflicted by her legal advisers could prove ruinous to your finances. At the least, after representations to your publishers, the book would be withdrawn from sale and your career with that house would be stillborn.

In this hypothetical case you should note that your publisher will not stand beside you. In your contract you have undertaken that your work is free from libel and, in an instance like this, you alone must take the blame. If the typescript you delivered had contained defamatory remarks about a public person or institution then the editor would have a chance to rectify the matter. But if you libel an individual known only to you, the publisher has no means of spotting the danger. Vigilance is mandatory – there are no excuses.

It is more likely, of course, that you may defame somebody unwittingly – erotic fiction has that potential. The disclaimer that often appears on the copyright page of the printed book – along the lines of 'All characters in this publication are fictitious and any resemblance to real persons, living or dead, is purely coincidental' – has no legal standing. In practice, however, the risk is negligible. Provided you take honest precautions to eliminate living people from your cast of characters, then you have a solid defence.

Rule nine then: Don't include recognisable characters.

Blasphemy

Geoffrey Robertson and Andrew Nicol's *Media Law* defines blasphemy as an offence that 'relates to outrageous comments about God, holy personages, or articles of the Anglican faith, and is constituted by vilification, ridicule or indecency.'

This may seem like a dead issue for any creative writer in that prosecution by the state is most unlikely – even though blasphemy remains a crime in the UK and most of the USA. There has not been a public prosecution under that law in England since 1922. Private prosecutions, however, cannot be ruled out. In 1977 *Gay News* and its editor were taken to court by that zealous defender of public morals, Mary Whitehouse, for publishing a poem that depicted Christ on the cross as a homosexual. The Whitehouse prosecution was successful and appeals to both the House of Lords and the European Court of Human Rights failed. Subsequently, the 1988 publication of Salman Rushdie's *The Satanic Verses* offended orthodox Muslims to the extent that he has lived life as a marked man ever since. He was not prosecuted – on a charge to which he would not have been able to mount a defence of literary merit – because the blasphemy law in England offers protection to the Anglican faith only.

These are deep waters and, no matter how amusing the idea, there is no point in paddling in them when writing a genre novel. The point to remember is that you do not necessarily have to offend against the law to draw down the wrath of individuals or groups of believers who may pursue you for redress.

Rule ten: Do not take the name of anybody's God in vain.

The Ten Commandments of erotica

1   No kids.
2   No dogs.
3   No corpses.
4   No excessive violence.
5   Handle drugs with care.
6   No incest.
7   Don't copy someone else's work without permission.
8   Don't quote from songs (unless you're prepared for a hassle).
9   Don't include recognisable characters.
10   No blasphemy.

10

YOU, THE AUTHOR

> 'Writing is easy; all you do is sit staring at a blank sheet
> of paper until the drops of blood form on your forehead.'
>
> Gene Fowler

Why do you want to write an erotic novel?

You will know the answer to that. At least, I hope you do. Unless you
are very secretive, your friends and family will put the question. You
might come up with one of these reasons:

1. It's practice for when I write my 'real' novel.

This is a good excuse to keep your friends off your back but don't
expect it to cut much ice in the publishing world when you come to
place a mainstream novel. Agents and publishers will not be
impressed to hear you have an erotic novel on sale or in your bottom
drawer. I'm not saying it will put them off but in their terms it's no
great achievement. For you, however, as an exercise in constructing a
full-length narrative – creating characters, telling a story, engaging
the reader's attention – writing erotica *is* a valid dry run for other
forms of fiction. If you complete it successfully, it is also a great confi-
dence-booster.

2. I'm just doing it for a laugh – but it could lead to something.

It's not easy to laugh all the way through 75,000 words – sense-of-
humour failure usually sets in at about the 15–20,000 mark. If you are
to complete an erotic novel, it will also take hard work and concentration. But it certainly could lead to something.

3. I've read some and they're all awful – I can do better.

As self-motivation this is fine. Don't tell your prospective publisher, however – he might publish those books that have earned your contempt.

4. I'm just doing it for the launch party and the chance to get on TV.

Sorry, you're in the wrong genre. You can, of course, pay for your own party out of the publication advance. And if you're female, prepared to slip into a slinky dress and will settle for cab-fare, you might get on to a late-night chat show on an obscure cable channel.

5. I like writing about sex

An excellent response and a good starting point for an erotic novelist – though you might have to think of something else to tell your mother-in-law.

6. I want to get rich.

Get real first. At the time of writing, the average advance for an erotic novel in the UK is around £2,000 (quite a lot less on some lists) and approximately $3,000 in the US. Even if you wrote one a month for year (nearly a million words – an impossible schedule for all but the most fluent) *and sold every one*, you'd end up a long way from real wealth. The standard advice is: Don't give up the day job.

7. I need some extra cash and I can write in the mornings when the kids are at school.

An unarguable response. I know many authors who plan their writing schedule around domestic duties and earn enough for the family holiday in the process. Creative writing, provided you can sell it, is an excellent part-time job for the house-bound.

> 'The answer to the question "why write about sex?" can only be a simple "why not?"'
>
> Derek Parker, *Writing Erotic Fiction* (1995)

Pseudonyms

Most erotica is written under a pseudonym and some writers have several. A smaller number write under their own names. What should you do?

This is, of course, a personal decision. I would say that you must have positive reasons in favour of revealing your identity. If you are sure that employing your real name would not cause embarrassment to your nearest and dearest, and if you are eager to promote yourself as an erotic writer, then maybe you should consider it. Authors who use their own names have a better chance of gaining publicity. By placing your own name on a work of erotica you stand up to be counted. It is interesting that, for the most part, it is authors of gay erotica who show their heads above the parapet.

Most erotic writers prefer to protect their privacy. One reason is obvious – few people are happy to admit to their daughter's head-mistress or the nosy-parker next door that they are the author of *Sex Sluts Go Wild in Leather*. However, there are other advantages to being coy about your identity. The literary world is a snobbish one and if you have any ambition to publish outside the erotic ghetto, your publisher will want to use an alternative name to the one on your erotica. In those circumstances I'm sure you, too, would want to publish your mainstream novels under your real name and keep the pseudonym for your sexy books.

A further advantage to a pseudonym is that you can take it on and off, like a hat. In fact, you can have a row of hats – many writers do. In this way, the successful erotic novelists write for many different publishers, with a separate pseudonym for each. Names can also be changed to suit series of books. Some writers are very flexible, producing different sequences in a variety of styles for several publishers. Over the years, these people accumulate a string of pen-names.

How do I choose a pseudonym?

There was a time, not so long ago, when all erotic novels were ascribed to 'Anonymous'. This was derived from the mass of Victorian pornography openly published (at last) in the 1970s and 1980s, whose authors really were anonymous. As a result, in the book trade, Anonymous became synonymous with 'dirty book'. Publisher's salesmen at the time would say, 'Let's have some more of that Anonymous' and publishers, naturally, supplied it, bringing out new work under that attribution. One advantage of this, from the bookseller's point of view, was that, when racked alphabetically by author, the erotica was placed on the top left-hand shelf, handily out of reach of under-age buyers. More to the point, those who wanted it knew exactly where to find it.

After the vogue for Anonymous, came the pseudonyms. They tended to contain surnames from the beginning of the alphabet, so that they too would be placed on that top shelf with all the other erotic books. Now, with space designated for erotica in most bookshops, this device is redundant. Consequently, you have a lot of leeway when choosing your pen name.

Selecting a pseudonym is like putting on a disguise. You can, for example, change your sex. Most pseudonyms are female though many of the writers are male. The theory is that male readers will be titillated by the thought of a woman recounting sexy deeds, whereas potential female readers will be put off by the thought of a male author. I can't say whether or not this is really the case. More to the point, maybe, is that a lot of erotica is written from a female character's point-of-view, often in the first person. It makes sense for these titles to appear to be written by a woman, whether they are or not.

So, you can see that your choice of a pen name will be affected by the nature of the book you've written. Leaving aside the gender issue, if your novel is called *Rendezvous in Roissy* you won't publish under the name of Trevor Fletcher or Moira Macrae or Ingrid Mortensen – you'll probably opt for something French. If you don't come to this conclusion, it's likely your publisher will.

It's possible you have a name in mind already, an amalgamation of your grandfather's middle name and your own maiden name, maybe, or an anagram of your surname and your nickname at school – something, at any rate, that has a personal connection. In which case, if you really seek anonymity, be careful that you don't give too many clues.

Writing space

In an ideal world, you would have exclusive use of a good-sized study with a desk and a chair, the most up-to-date computer equipment and a personal assistant to shield you from interruptions and bring you regular refreshment. In reality, you may be struggling with a notebook and a pencil on the corner of the kitchen table surrounded by family and pets all demanding your attention.

Many books have been written on the kitchen table but the task is easier when you have use of the study. So, what is essential?

Computers

'To err is human, but to really foul things up requires a computer.'

Anonymous

You need some means of printing your work to submit to a publisher, for no editor will consider longhand. In the worst case an old type-writer will do but, unpalatable though it is to a vociferous Luddite minority, a word-processing programme is ten times better. At the top end of the scale, a CD-ROM and a modem for access to the Internet can make research a seductive pleasure. What counts though is to be able to arrange the words on screen to your satisfaction and print them out cleanly.

If you are sharing a computer you must file your work carefully. Given the nature of your writing, I would suggest that the ability to pass-word-protect your files would be useful, particularly if sharing the machine with youngsters. Knowing that your files cannot be accessed by anyone else gives both peace of mind and makes it easier to shed your inhibitions on screen.

Computers are marvellous writing aids. They can cut and paste copy, reproduce it in an endless variety of fonts and formats, and achieve complex revisions at the touch of a key. But, if you possess one, I'm sure you won't make the mistake of trusting it completely. Apart from backing up copy separately on a regular basis and always keeping a spare print cartridge, there can be unexpected pitfalls:

> Oh, the joys of editing on computer. Except, of course, when the dear old PC doesn't see what the human mind sees. John Rowe Townsend, at a recent Independent Publishers Guild meeting, told a story as proof of this. The editors decided they didn't like the name David for the lead character in a novel; they wanted something more down to earth, like Fred. A few touches on the computer's buttons resolved this problem and all worked well until the hero and heroine took a trip to Florence in chapter twelve. 'Gazing in awe at Michelangelo's *Fred*' did not have quite the right ring to it.
>
> *Bookseller*, 31/1/97

This is a cautionary tale of special significance to any erotic novelist who decides at the last minute the male protagonist should not be called Dick.

Privacy

You may be different, but most authors I know prefer to marshal their thoughts in private. This is particularly true of erotic authors. If your mind is focused on an intimate moment of physical passion you don't want to be interrupted by your children chucking paint around or your flatmates watching soaps on the TV. If the only space available is communal then you must use it when everyone else is out or asleep – there's no alternative. This may seem daunting but if you are serious about writing you will find some way of doing it. Think of your erotic novel as a weed – resilient, persistent and able to flourish in the most unpromising conditions. Some weeds, though reviled, are also beautiful.

Reference books

Here, the sky's the limit and it does depend exactly what you plan to write. In my opinion, only two reference works are essential – a dictionary and a thesaurus, both of which are commonly found as standard items in word-processing packages. Next in line, I'd put a baby names' book and a concise dictionary for writers and editors – the kind that includes common foreign-language words, abbreviations, punctuation difficulties and so on. Naturally a guide to English usage, an atlas, a dictionary of slang and many more works may be of use – you could spend a fortune, especially if you've got that CD-ROM. If you are short of money and space, stick to the basics and take a list of queries to the library.

A novel with a historical setting might require some relevant background texts. Reference works on clothing can be useful for the erotic novelist – particularly those that deal with period undergarments. Also – and here's justification for that stash of porno publications you keep under the bed – some magazines with explicit photographs of naked men and women. In this genre you must be able to describe a variety of attractive bodies in detail. It may help you to have the kind of visual reference on hand that a dirty magazine can provide. When you buy it, you can say in all honesty to those in the queue behind you, 'It's for research.'

Who to tell

You may not care who knows of your writing intentions or you may even keep them secret from your partner. Some authors like to talk about their work in progress, others would rather cut their throats – whatever the nature of their work. For the most part, authors are proud to discuss their books and their friends and family are curious and supportive. That may not be the case with you and your erotic novel.

Only you can make an informed guess as to how your project will be received and who you tell about it is up to you. But it is important that you think about exactly who to confide in because once the genie is out of the bottle he will not go back in. If, for example, you do not want the people you live with to know that you have sold an erotic novel your publisher will be sympathetic and make arrangements to contact you on your own terms. You will have to supply a contact phone number and, if possible, a third-party address. Provided the editor can get hold of you and is briefed as to your circumstances, there is no reason why your cover should be blown. In other words, rest easy – your mother need not know.

11

SEEKING PUBLICATION

'Writing is the only profession where no one considers you ridiculous if you earn no money.'

Jules Renard

First steps

In an ideal world, your first step takes place before you write a line and probably before you invent any firm plot ideas. It is simply to visit a bookshop and study the erotica shelves.

The purpose of your trip is to discover your target publishers – those who publish erotica, preferably in a list dedicated to the genre. After all, it would be pointless to send your book to a firm that does not sell sexy books. If you consult publishing reference works, such as *The Writers' and Artists' Yearbook*, you may well be overwhelmed by the number of publishing houses and will have to sift through a lot of unnecessary information. There's no substitute for browsing the shelves yourself and getting the feel – literally – of the books on offer.

Compile a list of publishers with erotic imprints. I could do it for you in this book but the chances are that the scene will have changed by the time you come to submit your material. You want up-to-date information and you can get it simply by looking at what's on sale.

Some publishers print a notice in their books inviting submissions from readers. Among other things, this will tell you the amount of material that is required and where it should be sent – which is what you need to know. If there is no 'Message from the Publisher', turn to the copyright page (at the beginning of the book, on the reverse of the title page) and make a note of the publisher's address.

Step two is to write to all the publishers on your list and simply ask for their guidelines for erotic submissions. There's no need to say anything at this stage about your project but you must enclose post-age for the reply. The response you get, which will vary from a page-length note to a dozen pages of detailed requirements (Black Lace are very generous), will be crucial to the successful completion of your ambitions.

Publishers' guidelines

Read publishers' guidelines carefully and take note of what they say. If a publisher asks for submissions of full-length novels between 70,000 and 80,000 words in length, don't send short stories or novels that run to only 60,000 words. Publishers won't trim their cloth to suit you, it's you who must do the trimming.

In all probability, the publisher will request a synopsis of your story and a decent portion of the content, at least 10,000 words. The guide-lines will also indicate the nature of the preferred material – in other words, if they favour SM material or don't welcome submissions from men, they will say so. You, of course, will know the kind of books they like because you will have examined some of their offerings currently on sale.

Submissions

Jumping ahead in the process, let's assume you sent off for guidelines when you first decided to write your book. Now you've written it – or written enough of it to provide the material your target publishers request. If you've completed the whole thing, you can either send it all off – but provide a synopsis as well – or (the cheaper, less time-consuming option) send the opening section to the requested length together with an outline. If you've only written the necessary sample you are, of course, hoping to get a commission to write the rest. Incidentally, if you are an unpublished writer it is rare to be commissioned by a publisher. Nevertheless it does happen in this genre, so go for it. At the very least you might get sufficient encouragement to finish your book and a friendly editorial contact into the bargain.

Send your material, including an SAE or sufficient postage to cover the possibility of return, together with a letter. This should be very simple, along the lines of:

Dear Blue Desire Books

I would like to submit my novel, *The Garter of Lady Godiva*, for consideration. I enclose an outline and an extract of 15,000 words, as requested in your guidelines.

I look forward to hearing from you when you have had an opportunity to read my material.

Yours faithfully

Harriet Hose

Only add other information if it is relevant – for example, if you have had work published elsewhere, or if there is something about you that can be exploited to aid sales of the book:

PS You may like to know that my sister hosts the Midnight Moments chat show on Friday night, which has viewing figures of ten million. (She says I can plug the book on the programme provided I ride naked round the studio on a horse – I'm game!)

There's no need to bang on for pages in your submission letter, state the pertinent facts and sign off.

Top ten don'ts of submission

1 Don't claim your book is brilliant and wonderful (leave the editor to

discover that for him/herself); or say your friends all tell you it's brilliant and wonderful (what else would they say?).

2 Don't denigrate the publisher's list – 'I've read some of the books you publish and they're crap'. Bear in mind the person reading your letter very likely decided to publish that crap in the first place.

3 Don't denigrate the genre – 'On 1 January this year I embarked on what I consider to be my magnum opus on Western philosophy and now I find I have a shortfall in my cash flow. Accordingly I intend to knock off a couple of so-called erotic novels in tandem with my serious work.' This writer is too pompous to write erotica.

4 Don't spin a sob story. You may be dying of a wasting disease but the editor won't like your book any better because he or she feels sorry for you – quite the contrary, in fact.

5 Don't say you'll do anything to get published, for example, accept a nominal advance. Just as there's no need to boast (see 1) you shouldn't sell yourself short.

6 Don't ask for a rundown of advances, print runs and contractual terms. The editor will discuss these matters in detail if and when the book is accepted.

7 Don't make sloppy spelling errors or use unnecessary inverted commas and capitals, such as 'I look forward to recieving your 'opinion' of my Novel.' The editor will not be impressed.

8 Don't send sample pages selected at random from throughout the book. It's impossible to judge text that does not run on consecutively.

9 Don't staple, bind or paperclip your material together. Just make sure it's numbered consecutively, typed on one side of the paper only, with double spacing and wide margins, and is secured with a rubber band.

10 Don't include your impression of the cover design. This is grounds for instant rejection.

Naturally, you should keep a copy of anything you send out and a record of when and where you sent it. Never, at any point in the publishing process, allow your only copy of original material to leave your hands.

Must I submit exclusively to one list at a time?

I don't think so but some editors can get sniffy about this, expecting all material to be offered on an exclusive basis unless stated otherwise. Personally, I think it sounds pretentious to offer an unsolicited book 'on exclusive' – that's what literary agents say when they're trying to persuade an editor to respond quickly. With respect, you are not in that position and the implied threat that you will show the book elsewhere unless you have a decision within a certain time-frame will cut no ice. The fact is, your book may well sit on a shelf, with piles of other submissions, before it is assessed. In these circumstances, you are at liberty to offer it to whoever you like.

Some publishers will acknowledge receipt of your material but you cannot bank on it. My advice would be to include with your letter, not only sufficient postage to cover the cost of return, but also a stamped, self-addressed postcard and request that it be posted back to you once your submission has arrived. I would then resist contacting the publisher for a month, six weeks even, if your patience stretches that far. After that you are quite entitled to ring up and ask when you can expect a response.

Rejection

It's happened to us all. Some people paper the walls with their rejection letters and still find a publisher in the end. Rejections come in a variety of forms, most of them short and anodyne. If you are lucky, you may get a specific comment or two and a reason why your book didn't fit the bill. If this happens to you, take note of what is said in a positive spirit. There is no point in contesting the decision. Writing a vituperative letter complaining that the editor has got the wrong end of the stick is only going to alienate a possible outlet for future projects. No editor likes to be told she's talking out of her rear end *even if she is*.

The chances are your rejection will say something like: 'Thank you very much for letting us look at your novel, *The Blonde in Black*, but after careful consideration we have come to the conclusion it is not one for us.' Or, it's 'not strong enough for our list' or 'too similar to another project we are planning' etc. Or the letter may say that the list in question is already well bought-up and that consequently the editor is being particularly rigorous in her acquisition of new titles. There may be references to the current state of the market ('competitive', 'unforgiving', 'tough to crack' – it always is).

Though valid, all these are polite let-downs that have the advantage of not being too specific. Editors learn early in their careers not to write rejection letters that say things like: 'I found the Paris scenes stimulating and evocative – what a pity the middle section switches to Hull.' If the editor writes a letter like this, ten to one the book will be back on her desk within the month with a note from the author saying: 'I've relocated the Hull section to Paris as you requested and now look forward to receiving your offer for publication.'

Editors won't give you chapter-and-verse on why your book is being turned down (even though you have asked for it) because there's nothing in it for the publishing company. Once the editor has decided that the book won't do, her interest evaporates immediately – but there remains the chore of writing the rejection letter, which, experience dictates, should be brief and polite. From an editor's point of view, there's no point in telling a writer his characters are unconvincing, his dialogue is wooden and the entire plot is dead in the water. A professional assassin doesn't waste bullets on a corpse.

Authors often consider themselves unlucky to be turned down – and with justification on occasions. If the editor has just bought a Roman orgy series she won't want your *I, Claudia*, no matter that it is much better researched and twice as horny. Similarly, if she has acquired all the titles she needs for the next two years, she'll be rejecting everything that crosses her desk, even from her regular authors. And sometimes your submission will simply push the anathema button. As an editor, I have frequently read material that I might have taken on if only the sample hadn't featured one of my pet hates. If, for example, you submitted to me a novel that opened with a Mile-High-Club bonk, a scene of the heroine appraising her nude body in a mirror ('not *bad* for her age, mused Samantha') or a dream sequence, I'd probably reject out of personal prejudice no matter how brilliant your treatment. Though the genre is fraught with the perils of *déjà lu*, these particular scenarios fill me with dread. You are not to know that, however – you've just been unlucky. Don't feel hard-done-by. Try a different publisher.

There's one thing you must realise about being rejected: unless you receive specific indications to the contrary, an editorial no – no matter how politely expressed – means just that. Even if you rewrite it, don't bother the publisher with the project again. Take any precise criticisms on board when you write your next book – perhaps the editor will buy that one instead.

The good – and bad – news

In this genre, first-time writers have a better chance of getting a sale than in any other. From your point of view, this is highly satisfactory. I wish I could say that the reason for this is that publishers and booksellers are keen to encourage new erotic writers. In fact, the real cause is that the book trade doesn't much care who writes the words between the sexy cover photo and the titillating blurb on the back. In erotica, it is the cover design and the availability of the book that determines what will sell, as opposed to the allure of the author. Accordingly, it doesn't matter if you haven't written one before – if the editor thinks your book can be packaged attractively, she'll buy it.

In fact, most books achieve the same kind of sales figures within a list. And though each list has its 'star' authors, they do not comprehensively outsell their peers – as happens in every other genre you can think of. John Grisham sells more courtroom dramas, Stephen King more horror novels and Dick Francis more horse-racing thrillers than any other writer in their respective fields. I'm not saying they don't have big-league competition but, compared to the average contender (certainly the newcomers) in their genre, they outsell them many times over. This is not the case in erotic fiction. As a result, most authors on a list tend to earn the same amount of money per title.

One incentive for an editor to buy your novel is that she can offer a first-time author less generous terms than an experienced writer.

Don't be dismayed by this. The chances are that what you don't get by way of upfront money you will earn later in royalties. The salient point is that this puts you, as a first-timer, at an advantage in getting published.

Do I need a literary agent?

The quick answer is no. Most erotic novels are acquired on standard terms that will not vary, whoever submits the material and negotiates the contract.

However, there are many valid reasons for an erotic author to seek representation. An agent, by definition, is on your side. While an editor could and should be sympathetic to your point of view, his or her salary is paid by the publishing house. The agent's money comes from commission on the author's sales. In an ideal publishing scenario – which does exist, honestly – the editor is the author's friend inside the publishing house while the agent is a friend outside it. Needless to say, it can be advantageous sometimes to have a friend on the outside.

You will have to pay for this friendship, of course – probably at a rate of ten or twelve and a half per cent of your earnings. You may not think this worth it if you simply intend to write the occasional erotic novel to supplement your income. But if you have the skills to write other kinds of books, or TV scripts or movie screenplays – in other words, if you have ambitions beyond the genre for a literary career – then a good agent is well worth the price.

Finding an agent can be as problematic as finding a publisher. You are unlikely to raise much interest by sending an agency a synopsis and sample of your unpublished erotic novel. On the other hand, if you succeed in placing your novel you will be in a better position to find representation. You will need to amass your ideas, both in and outside the genre, and use your published novel as proof that you are a marketable proposition. Literary agents are listed in publishing reference works such as the *Writers' and Artists' Yearbook*, for the UK, and in *LMP* (*Literary Market Place*) for the USA. Which one do you choose? Unless you know of someone firsthand – maybe through a local writers' group – I'd suggest you stick a pin in the list and be prepared for a lot of rejections.

12

BEING PUBLISHED

> 'Almost anyone can be an author; the business is to collect money and fame from this state of being.'
>
> A. A. Milne

Acceptance

Let's assume that your hard work has paid off and at the first – or ninety-first – time of asking your submission has caught a publisher's fancy. You'll probably receive a phone call from the editor followed by a letter confirming the offer for publication.

In this call, the editor will undoubtedly say what she likes about your book, puff her list and say how your book would fit into it. If changes are required the editor will say so at this stage – whether it's a simple matter (a new title) or a more complex one (fewer scenes at the benefit office, more whipping and cut the anorexia). You will be asked if you have a literary agent. If you don't, you'll be offered the standard deal for newcomers; if you do, the editor will phone the agent and haggle. You don't have to accept a proposal on the spot. In fact, it makes sense to listen to what the editor has to say, even to ask to see a blank contract form, before committing yourself.

> 'OK, Caro, you're on. We'll pay you two thousand pounds advance against royalties.'
>
> 'God, darling, can't you do better than that?'
>
> 'I thought you needed money?'

> 'I don't call two grand money, I call it an insult.'
>
> *Lust on the Line*, Noel Amos (1996)

In all probability you will agree to the offer the editor proposes. What choice do you have the first time out? The answer is, not much. However, you are entitled to ask if these are the best terms available and to try to improve them. Whatever your feelings, treat the editor's proposal with respect and maintain your good humour. And ask questions, such as 'What's the publication date?', 'How many copies will you print?', 'What will the book cost in the shops?', 'Will I see the cover before it goes to press?', 'Can I approve the blurb?' As you can see, there are other significant factors, apart from the money, in a publishing deal. All of these are enshrined in the contract.

Vanity presses

On a cautionary note, do not confuse an offer from a publisher with a proposal from a vanity press. It may be that you have sent your book in answer to an advertisement soliciting new writers. If this is followed by a 'Congratulations, your work has been accepted' letter or call, don't reach for the champagne just yet. Listen to the suggestion that is made to you. If the publisher proposes to manufacture and sell your book at his expense and pay you royalties or a fee for doing so, then that is a legitimate offer. If, on the other hand, he suggests that you make a contribution to the cost of producing the book then that is a different order of business. If you are desperate to see your work in print and have a few thousand pounds you don't mind saying goodbye to, then you may wish to proceed. Just don't kid yourself you are being published in the accepted sense of the term. Bona fide publishers pay their authors, not the other way round.

Contracts

Here's a subject worthy of a book in itself. However, I'll try to make this section concise. This book was not intended to be a cure for insomnia.

Publishers' contracts vary in length, from a page or so to a couple of dozen. If you are a British author writing for a UK publisher, with luck you will be offered an agreement that conforms to certain minimum terms and conditions agreed by the publisher with The Society of Authors and The Writers' Guild of Great Britain. This is known as an MTA – minimum terms agreement – and, as the phrase implies, is a guarantee of basic standards.

The contract lays down in a legally binding form the obligations of the author and the publisher. In it, the publisher commits to publishing the Work (as your novel is referred to) at its own expense, within a certain time frame (usually twelve months from receipt of the complete typescript) for which it will pay you, the author, a percentage of the money received from sales of the book (royalties). As a rule, money is paid to the author in advance of publication in expectation of royalty earnings (the advance). This advance, it should be noted, is said to have 'earned out' when the royalties from sales exceed the money already paid. Frequently – much more frequently in the literary mainstream, where substantial sums can change hands – the advance never earns out. If this happens, the author does not have to pay the money back.

When you sign the contract as an author you promise that your book is all your own work, that you own the copyright in it (which you do by virtue of having written it), that you are free to offer it for publication (that is, you haven't sold it to anyone else), that you will deliver at the stipulated length on the agreed date, that it's not libellous or otherwise liable to land you in court (see Chapter 9) and that you grant the publisher the right to exploit the property in a multitude of ways. These include selling your book in specified formats in certain territories of the world and arranging with third parties – foreign language publishers, newspapers, film and television companies, audio-book companies – the right to publish in their respective formats and territories.

This whole area of secondary exploitation is known as subsidiary rights. In effect, if you grant the publisher your subsidiary rights you are appointing the firm as your agent to sell them on your behalf. In which case, it is worth noting that large publishers employ staff specifically to sell these rights; small firms either add it to the workload of a staffer or, sometimes, employ a specialist freelance. In practice, your best hope of earning additional income this way is from a foreign language sale and sales to a book club. It's well worth asking about this aspect of the proposed arrangement and looking closely at the percentages you would earn from any sub rights deals.

There are other clauses in a publishing contract covering the precise nature of the advance pay-out, royalty levies, accounting timetables, free copies and the termination of the agreement. Though formally worded, much of it is self-explanatory. The following matters, however, are worth explaining to the uninitiated.

Proofs

Proofs are the typeset but unbound pages of a book that must be read through for errors and marked up for correction. A novel is a straight-forward production task – unlike, for example, a reference work with integrated illustrations – and requires only one proof stage. The contract requires the author to read and correct within a certain time scale, probably three weeks. It also points out that it may charge the author for excessive alterations – a necessary safeguard against the author who treats proofs as a first draft. It's important that you get your book as right as you can before you deliver in the first place. Rewriting at proof will make you very unpopular with your publisher and might land you with a bill.

Option

An option clause grants the publisher first refusal of the author's next book 'of a similar nature' (or some such wording). You will probably be more than happy to sign it, for you, like the publisher, are looking forward to a long-term association. If you are writing under a pseudonym, I would suggest you ensure the clause refers to you 'writing as Giselle Labelle' (or whatever). This wording leaves you free to write for other erotic lists under other pen names – which could be handy.

Cover approval

This may not be part of the contract you are offered. Even if it is, you won't get the right to veto the cover design, though you should be offered the opportunity to have your say. If the matter is not mentioned at all, you should seek reassurance that you will be given the chance to air your opinion before it is too late – 'consultation' is the term publishers use. A decent contract should commit to showing you proposed cover treatments and the accompanying words (cover copy/blurbs) in time for you to say what you think of them. Your views may well be ignored but the publisher will be forced to produce reasons for doing so. And it's better than receiving a monstrosity through the post and being told, 'It's too late to change it now, we've printed enough for the entire run.'

Word count

Publishers talk a lot about word count, though it is a very approximate measure of the length of a printed book. However, it is a useful yardstick as to your progress and contracts generally specify that the book you deliver must be so many thousands of words.

If you are writing on a computer, the word-processing software will be able to tell you exactly how much you have written, down to the last word. You can even set up your screen to copy a printed page in a book, though book settings vary. Bear in mind that a computer word count won't take into account the fact that dialogue uses up many more lines than the equivalent number of words in a section of prose. New chapters also take up extra space in a printed book. All-in-all, the computer is a hard taskmaster and underestimates the amount of room your work will require on the printed page. If your machine tells you've reached 70,000 words and your contract asks for 75,000, I'd say you've reached the finishing line – on a strict word- count basis. If at that stage you still have to foil the villain, stage the orgy at the The Tit-Clamp Club and allow the heroine to land her man in a culminating, no-holds-barred night of lust on the Orient Express, then you know you'll have to do some pruning. With luck, if you've been keeping an eye on the wordage as you progress, you won't be in this position.

If you don't have access to software that counts for you then you will have to do it yourself. Take four pages from the script and count the words they contain, then divide by four to find an average page length. Multiply that figure by the number of pages you have written to see how far you've got. Frankly, you don't need to count every word. You can soon discover the average number of words in a line and multiply that by the lines on the page.

Check that the number of lines per page is consistent throughout your typescript, also that your margins do not vary. If you've swapped between typewriters or word-processors you will have to make the necessary allowances. A new chapter should begin on an new page. If you have divided your book into parts as well as chapters you should allow for this too.

All this is less complicated to do than to describe. All you really need to find out is the average length of one of your finished pages, the rest is simple arithmetic. Don't drive yourself crazy – this is not an exact science.

Preparing material for delivery

Produce your book on plain A4 or $8^{1}/_{2}$ x 11-inch paper, with generous margins and line spacing. For preference, make the type 12 point, it's easy on the eye. Present your work in a way that makes it as reader-friendly as possible, so don't use a failing print cartridge or a faded typewriter ribbon. Editors – readers in general, in fact – don't like to look at a dense, closely typed page of text. They also don't appreciate a page of fancy typefaces and background shading – which is a pity if you enjoy playing with your new turbo-charged word-processing software. Use one plain font and italicise when you have to. Don't underline – unless you can't italicise your typeface – and don't make the face bold.

Beyond catering for the jaded editorial eye, there is another reason to provide margins and line spacing. Once accepted, editorial amendments will be made directly on to your printed-out pages. Additions, alterations and copy-editing marks can be made more easily and legibly when the page is not covered from top to bottom in close-packed type.

You might be wondering why, if you have written your book on a computer and saved it to disk, anyone should want to work on your hard copy. Wouldn't it be easier for the publisher to make the changes on screen and print from the corrected disk? Maybe, but this isn't how it works – at present, anyway. For one thing, it is hard to read a novel on a computer screen. And if the editor edited the book that way, there would be no record of your original version, which can be important (particularly to you). In practice, editing work should be done on your printed copy and in pencil (so it can be erased if necessary). The typesetter may then use your disk – it saves a basic keying-in process – but will have to transfer the editor's corrections from the edited hard copy. It's a standard joke in publishing that, though the new technology points towards the paperless office, publishers spend their time poring over vast hills of the darn stuff. And the finished typescript an author provides, which is subsequently edited by hand, is the key document in the whole process.

The publisher's point of view

Publishers, whatever they may say, are in business to make money. Put it another way, unless they make money there is no business. The best of them have a vision of the books they want to publish to make that money and, given the chance, they will offer high-sounding mission statements about their purpose. But no matter how elevating – and sincere – these pronouncements, there's no getting away from the fact that general (as opposed to academic) publishing is a gambling business. Commercial books, in particular, are like steeple-chasers – no matter how well backed they can still fall over and not all runners finish in the frame. One of the attractions of erotic publishing is that it generates cash while operating outside the high-risk horse race of frontlist publishing.

Of recent years the lists dedicated to erotic books have provided a reliable income for their publishers without a lot of the hassle that goes with more visible publishing, such as high advances, marketing expense and the consumption of publicity time (not to mention the massaging of author egos). And, traditionally, erotic books are not subject to the same level of returns as other categories of fiction (for the most part, the book trade operates on a sale-or-return basis – if the book doesn't sell, the bookshop returns it to the publisher). Of course, things can change and if erotica loses its status as a 'nice little earner' then publishers will look with less favour on this part of their programme.

The editor

Publishing companies of any size are comprised of several different departments with separate functions. Between Editorial (which acquires the books) and Sales (which sells them) – the beginning and the end of the publishing process – there's Production (book manufacture), the Art Department (jacket and cover design), Subsidiary Rights (rights selling), Marketing (paid-for promotion) and Publicity (free promotion), not to mention Accounts, Personnel and other layers of bureaucracy.

From your point of view, the editor *is* the publisher and your guide to the whole business. The editor's job is to acquire books for his or her list and to see them through the often-lengthy birthing process that is publication. Editors are the midwives in the business of book gestation and they'll do what they can to smooth matters along.

On average, it takes around nine to twelve months from delivery of a typescript to publication – though this varies from publisher to publisher. One reason for this is that books are presented and sold to the main customers (book chains, wholesalers, supermarkets) many months ahead of publication. The process can, of course, happen much quicker but there's usually a good reason for that – a biography of a pop star is rushed through to cash in on current popularity or a thriller from a mega-star author is brought forward in the schedule to meet this year's sales target. As you can imagine, an erotic novel is not likely to be produced on a crash time-scale.

The editor will assess and acknowledge your book on delivery and discuss any textual queries that may arise. In general, he or she will keep you informed of progress on your book. Very likely you'll forge a bond of friendship through your phone calls and exchange of notes. On the whole, publishing is a congenial business and editors are happy to chat once in a while. You might even, if you're lucky, get invited to a publishing lunch – though don't, these days, expect anything lavish.

It's not advisable, however, to let too much chumminess get in the way of what is important. Just as the editor will expect you to stick to your delivery date so you shouldn't be fobbed off when your royalty statement does not turn up on time. Things do go wrong in publishing – books go astray, names are misspelt in catalogues, cheques somehow fail to get signed – and the editor is the person who should sort these things out for you. In practice, you may find your editor elusive – there *are* a lot of meetings to attend (not to mention lunch). So here's a tip: always be particularly polite to the editor's assistant. Apart from the fact that one day the assistant may be the editor, he or she always knows how to pin the editor down.

Marketing and publicity

Cue hollow laughter from experienced authors – *what* marketing and publicity? they cry. This is an area where resources (human in particular) are stretched. For a publisher, there's never enough money and time – huge amounts of both can be spent to little effect. Publishers with lists of any size have to prioritise their efforts, and erotica is rarely a priority – though you may be lucky and have your book out at the time when the list itself is due for a promotional spend. Just don't hold your breath.

Self-promotion

Unless you write under your own name it is difficult for the publicity department to get you on TV and radio or find you space in the press. But, as previously mentioned, if you are not coy about your identity, then there may be possibilities. You can also, to some extent, take matters into your own hands.

Ask Publicity or your editor for a few extra copies of your book for review purposes and send them out to your local media. Invest in some good photographs and include one with the book, together with a press release you've cooked up yourself on your word-processor. Tell them a bit about yourself – past jobs or other experiences that contrast with the role of erotic novelist can make good copy for a desperate journalist. You know the kind of thing: 'Convent Girl Takes Up A New Habit', 'Night Nurse Sets The Pulse Racing', etc. Obviously, it helps if you are personable and, not so obviously, if you are female. The notion that women are capable of writing sexy books is still considered news in some quarters. Female authors who are prepared to come clean about their erotica are regularly featured in women's magazines and the so-called women's pages of newspapers. In this context, women who openly write erotica are applauded as empowering other women by putting them in touch with their sensuality. As for males... at the time of writing, you remain dirty old men. Sorry.

Other ideas for self-promotion: ask for the phone number of your publisher's local representative and get in touch. Find out from him or her who stocks erotica in your area and introduce yourself. It's unlikely any bookshop will want an erotic author for signing sessions but simply by making yourself known you should be able to persuade them to stock your book. (To be honest, these tactics work best with non-erotic work but it's worth a try – booksellers do like to know authors who live in their area.) You could also, though it may go against the grain, throw your own launch party and invite the local media for a few drinks. They might not show up but if you've got enough friends (and booze) on hand that needn't spoil the party.

Even if you are reluctant to stand up and shout from the rooftops that you write erotic books, there's another path you could pursue. If you have access to the Internet on your computer, why not create your own home page? This requires some expertise (such as knowing how to convert your text into HTML, or HyperText Markup Language, which you need to create web documents) and maybe some expense but, for the cyber-minded, it's worth thinking about. Get on to your Internet provider or buy a book on the subject, if this appeals to you. It would be a good way of blowing your trumpet under your writing name without blowing your cover.

One final word on this topic. Whatever you do, make sure your publisher's Publicity department know what you are up to. They'll be delighted and might even turn up to help you polish off the alcohol.

Covers

The cover of your novel is its primary selling tool. This is true of most original paperbacks but the visual appeal of an erotic novel has even more significance. One reason, already discussed, is that it is most unlikely to have any other exposure – no author tours, no signing sessions, no advertising. Another is that, in this genre, the author's track record counts for little. Even if you have already published half a dozen blistering novels in the same series, it is unlikely that you will find a retailer sufficiently interested in erotica to recognise your track record and stock your new title accordingly. Booksellers buy books like yours strictly on cover appeal. Then, once it's on the shelves, your novel must look sufficiently alluring to make a prospective purchaser pick it up in preference to those around it.

There's not much you can do about this state of affairs but you should be aware of the issues involved. The cover, hopefully with some input from you as already mentioned, is the publisher's responsibility.

Titles

You may feel that this matter – as opposed to the photograph or illustration on the cover – is exclusively your province. However, since the title of a book is crucial to its packaging, the publisher will want the last word. Titles are changed frequently in every genre and it's not uncommon for a publisher's forward schedule to be peppered with the word 'Untitled'. In your case, you may be wedded to one title and resistant to change but, if the publisher has a good reason to oppose *Sex Romps in the Suburbs* – 'sounds like non-fiction', 'books with "romp" in the title don't sell', 'we used that title last week' – you must look for an alternative. If the publisher hates it, don't fight the decision, put your energy into finding something you both like. That said, you are entitled to veto your editor's pet suggestion if you genuinely dislike it. If it had been left to Blanche Knopf (the publisher), so the story goes, Raymond Chandler's *Farewell, My Lovely* would have been called *Sweet Bells Jangle*.

What you can expect of your publisher

First of all, you can expect the company, whether a multinational conglomerate in a city skyscraper or one man and his computer in a garden shed, to abide by the terms of the contract. You should be consulted about editorial changes, be warned ahead of time when proofs are due so you can allocate time to read them, be shown cover designs and copy and, the most important item of all, *you should be paid on time.* Publishing is a shifting sands kind of business, every so often the winds change and the landscape is rearranged. Companies are bought and sold – and occasionally some go to the wall owing their authors money. If your company consistently fails to cough up when obliged to do so, this is could be a warning signal. In any event, they are in breach of contract and I wouldn't sell them any more books.

Apart from the strict letter of the publishing agreement, the author can expect from his publisher efficiency and courtesy – which is what he will expect in return. Provided both parties stick to the bargain they have struck, the working relationship can be almost entirely pleasurable. Unless you are going to self-publish – and you need another book to advise you about that courageous course of action – the author needs the publisher and vice-versa. 'Literature flourishes best when it is half a trade and half an art,' said W. R. Inge, the gloomy dean of St Paul's, who would probably not be amused to be quoted in this context. However, his words are as true of erotic literature as any other kind. So remember, if relations ever become strained with your publisher, *he's* the tradesman and *you're* the artist.

SOME USEFUL READING

Writing guides

Aspects of the Novel, E. M. Forster, Penguin (1927)
> The text of his famous Cambridge lectures. Accessible and valuable to all writers of fiction.

The Craft of Novel-Writing, Dianne Doubtfire, Allison & Busby (1978)
> Good practical advice. See also her *Teach Yourself Creative Writing*, Hodder & Stoughton (1983).

Writing the Novel: From Plot to Print, Lawrence Block, Writer's Digest Books (1986)
> Words of wisdom from a voice of experience.

Write Tight, William Brohaugh, Writer's Digest Books (1993)
> Subtitled 'How to keep your prose sharp, focused and concise'. Guaranteed to have you looking at your work with a fresh – and critical – eye.

Elements of Arousal, Lars Eighner, Richard Kasak Books (1994)
> Subtitled 'How to write and sell gay men's erotica', this is far more than that and is recommended to anyone who wants to write fiction of any kind.

A Manual of Writer's Tricks, David L. Carroll, Marlowe & Company (1995)
> Tips on style, neatly expressed.

Writing Erotic Fiction, Derek Parker, A & C Black (1995)

An elegantly written overview of the erotic genre, strong on the history of pornography.

Bestseller, Celia Brayfield, Fourth Estate (1996)

Brilliant insights into the creation of popular fiction by a best-selling writer with the perception to analyse her own gift.

Reference

Writers' and Artists' Yearbook, A & C Black

Annual publication stuffed with contact addresses – the book all publishers refer you to when they request you send your unsolicited novel elsewhere.

The Writer's Handbook, Macmillan

Similar to the above.

The Society of Authors

There is no trades union for erotic novelists but there is the Society of Authors, which, if you are a British writer, you can join either as a full member (if you have had a full-length work published) or as an associate (if you are in receipt of an offer to publish). I don't intend to write a commercial for the Society but you should be aware of the services they provide, particularly if you are not represented by an agent. They will, for example, vet members' contracts, take up an author's complaints and, in some circumstances, pursue legal redress on a writer's behalf. They publish short booklets on topics such as copyright in its various forms, authors' agents, income tax and so on, which are also available to non-members for a small fee (£2 at the time of writing). Contact The Society of Authors at 84, Drayton Gardens, London SW10 9SB. Phone: 0171 373 6642, fax 0171 373 5768. E-mail: authorsoc@writers.org.uk – it seems I wrote the commercial anyway.

THE EROTIC
ALPHABET

In case you should find yourself reading material peppered with indecipherable acronyms, or party to a conversation that excludes you by
the same token, the following may be of use.

A-levels	anal sex
B&D	bondage and discipline
Bi	bisexual
CP	corporal punishment
D&S	domination and submission
DIY	masturbation
DOM	dominant
O-levels	oral sex
SM/S&M	sadomasochism
SUB	submissive
TS	transsexual
TV	transvestite

INDEX

THE CREATIVE WRITING SERIES

What makes a good story into a publishable novel or a creative vision into the next award-winning screenplay? In this series, experienced authors in a wide range of creative writing genres share their knowledge and expertise to help aspiring authors find their voice. All the books in the series demonstrate how to develop ideas into a saleable form and give plenty of opportunities for practising newly acquired writing skills along the way – from the germ of an idea to a finished work.

Titles

Creative writing
Screenwriting
Writing a novel
Writing for children
Writing poetry
Writing erotic fiction
Writing a romantic novel
Writing fantasy and science fiction
Writing crime and suspense fiction
Writing essays and reports